"In this engaging journe_ the threads of a remar_ well-lived can have_ generations downstrean_ can turn the efforts of ordinary people into something of eternal value, ultimately impacting thousands of people across the globe."
**Jonathan Lamb, Minister-at-Large
of Keswick Ministries**

"The Quinta holds great memories for me, my family and our church when we retreated there over many Easters to seek God and bask in His presence. The story of The Quinta is an example of the transformational power of Christ Jesus at work. Its history is a Christ-centred testimony, providing lessons for navigating the successes and failures of life."
**Ade Omooba MBE, Director
of Christian Concern**

"As an account of the remarkable history of The Quinta, Peter's work is a tour de force. His weaving in of his own story adds colour and personality. Indeed, his sensitive and candid reflections may prove to be the most useful part of the book. His engagement with The Quinta has made him uniquely able to write its story. I am most thankful to him for doing so."
**Andrew Boulter, Chair of Trustees
of Centre Ministries**

"It is encouraging to read how the vision of one man in the nineteenth century to provide 'pleasant relaxation' for ministerial friends, coupled with a strong vision and support for mission, has led to an extraordinary ministry based at The Quinta that is still refreshing and equipping people for Christian service today."

Matthew Skirton, Former National Director of Operation Mobilisation UK and Quinta

AN UNBELIEVABLE INHERITANCE

A Journey Through The History Of The Quinta

Copyright © 2025 Peter Bevington

The moral right of the author has been asserted.

Apart from any fair dealing for the purposes of research or private study, or criticism or review, as permitted under Copyright, Design and Patents Act 1998, this publication may only be reproduced, stored or transmitted, in any form or by any means, with prior permission in writing of the publishers, or in any case of the reprographic reproduction in accordance with the terms of licences issued by the Copyright Licensing Agency. Enquiries concerning reproduction outside these terms should be sent to the publishers.

PublishU Ltd

www.PublishU.com

All Scripture Quotations are taken from THE MESSAGE, copyright © 1993, 2003, 2018 by Eugene H Peterson. Used by permission of NavPress. All rights reserved. Represented by Tyndale House Publishers.

All rights of this publication are reserved.

WELCOME

You are invited to join a fascinating journey of discovery.

You can learn how The Quinta became the place it is today.

You can enjoy the stories of people touched by this place by looking through their eyes and entering their emotions. Their experience can inform, challenge and encourage anyone seeking personal meaning and purpose.

Your Itinerary

Chapter 1: What's In a Name?
Chapter 2: The Wild West Show; Land, Wealth and Power
Chapter 3: An Inspirational Life
Chapter 4: A Remarkable Woman
Chapter 5: Death and the Seeds of Life
Chapter 6: Fruit in the Wilderness
Chapter 7: Waiting for the Future; Living in the Present
Chapter 8: An Open Door
Chapter 9: Resourced to Serve
Chapter 10: Freed to Serve
Chapter 11: A Cast of Thousands
Chapter 12: Fireside Reflections

Your Guide

Peter Bevington became a temporary Housemaster for Dr Barnardo's at The Quinta School in 1971. He joined the teaching staff a year later and stayed until the school closed in 1980. After working for Leicestershire Social Services, he returned for another temporary appointment to open the new Quinta Christian Centre on 4 July 1985 with his wife Jenni, son Tim and son Matt, who was born five months later. Temporary again became permanent. Peter and Jenni stayed until 2014 when Peter retired. This half-century of experience qualifies him to guide you on your journey as he uncovers the past and reports the stories of many others.

What to Expect

Your journey will be like walking along a river from source to sea. In this type of walk, it is a joy to take in not only the villages, towns and cities but also to absorb the flow of the river: its rapids, backwaters and even the way it shapes its own environment. Its atmosphere seeps into the soul as one fully assimilates the journey's impact.

Your invitation is to journey likewise, but through the history of The Quinta over the past two centuries. History merges with mystery. So much is unknown. Questions of intention and feeling are often unanswered. The journey will celebrate success but not avoid engaging with painful places. As you reflect on what you discover, I invite you to consider the more profound questions of meaning and purpose and the impact of faith.

The initial focus of this journey is a place, The Quinta. But a place without people is dead, and people without purpose are meaningless. As the journey progresses, underlying questions emerge. What is the "river" that we are following? Is it the place, is it the people or will it turn out to be something entirely different?

'An Unbelievable Inheritance' is a remarkable story. If you decide that it is believable, then what are the implications of that? As your guide, I pray that your journey through life will be blessed by this journey through the history of The Quinta.

Please Come Equipped

History is personal. What we see and understand is interpreted by our own prejudices. Just consider watching a match. Your "history" of the game will be quite different from the "history" written by the opposing supporters.

In this virtual journey, please trade in your walking boots and wet weather clothing for discerning headgear, eyes that see, ears that hear and emotions that engage. Pack an open mind and a readiness to explore new ideas and places.

Excess baggage should be left behind. As you look back on lives without modern technologies, be prepared to set aside twenty-first-century arrogance. Please substitute condemnation for humility.

Your Fellow Travellers

As your guide, I am deeply grateful to Jenni, my immediate and extended family and my friends. They made this guide possible and held my hand on my personal journey through part of the real-time Quinta story. There are so many others involved. A special thanks to those in this group of wonderful people whose stories are featured and who have made special efforts to help create this guide. Almost all those mentioned are referred to only by their Christian names. This is deliberate to emphasise that these stories are of ordinary people. All contributions are dedicated to Jesus, the ultimate guide, who described Himself as "the Way, the Truth and the Life" (John 14:6).

Before You Start, Essential Information About The Quinta

For those unfamiliar with The Quinta, the following basic facts may be helpful: The Quinta is a small 52-acre parkland estate in northwest Shropshire, on the English border of the Welsh hills. It hosts the UK headquarters of Operation Mobilisation (OM). This large international missionary society provides mission, training and relief work worldwide in over 145 nations, with 4,500 staff members from 125 countries. They also have two ships that constantly visit ports worldwide, wherever they can gain access.[1]

The Quinta is held in Trust, and the Trustees use the estate for one of the UK's larger Christian conference centres, with six units catering for groups of any size, up to 280, and accommodating over 1,000 if camping is included. Although full-board options are available, it specialises in offering value-for-money, self-catering and activities for families and young people.[2]

Almost every person who knows The Quinta's present will not be aware of all the details of its past: how the shadows of the future can be found in the light of The Quinta's past. The complete story of The Quinta is told here for the first time. The full panorama revealed in this journey is truly remarkable. It resonates and reverberates like a masterful work of fiction. This story of an unbelievable inheritance must be told and demands to be read.

WHAT'S IN A NAME?

The journey starts with the question that everyone asks: "Where did the name, 'Quinta' come from?"

Answers require some knowledge of local history and geography.

Apart from one early reference, it is as though The Quinta appears from nowhere around 1800.

Chirk Castle

Chirk Aqueduct & Viaduct

Oak at the Gate of the Dead

QUINTA TIMELINE 1850 1900

Chapter 1
What's In a Name?

When I first arrived in 1971, The Quinta was considered remote. The area was once described as one of the few remaining "rural idylls" in the UK. It was seen as a place where you could escape the rush of modern life and enjoy the traditional countryside surrounding the market town of Oswestry. But that is not the whole picture. The area is located on the edge of the Shropshire Plain, adjacent to the Welsh Hills, near the northern end of the Welsh Borders. It has an extensive military history.

The leading explanation for its unusual name is that a former owner had travelled abroad and anglicised the name "La Quinta" directly from the Spanish or Portuguese for a country house or villa. This is both obvious and plausible. However, I have found that this theory has sometimes been ascribed to the first person named as the owner of The Quinta, Frederick West. He was born in 1767 and owned The Quinta at the beginning of the nineteenth century. However, he cannot have introduced the name because a record from the accounts of the neighbouring Chirk Castle Estate in 1686 shows The Quinta listed as a "gentleman's residence".[3] The name must have been introduced earlier if this theory is correct. Other theories are only possible if you dig deeper and open your mind to different ideas by better understanding the area. If I take a map and a compass and draw a three-mile circle around Quinta Hall, it is impressive how much lies within that radius. Old Oswestry Hill Fort is three miles to the south of The Quinta. It was built and occupied during the Iron Age (800 BC to 43 AD) and is one of the best-preserved hillforts in Britain.

Even closer, to the east of The Quinta, in the dry summer of 1976, crop markings captured by aerial photography suggested a Roman encampment. Excavations in 1977 showed the remains of a well-preserved military site that was used and reused throughout the Roman occupation of Britain. Archaeologists were amazed to discover that the camps, an earlier and a later one, covered about 42 acres.[4]

Within the circle are the remains of two motte and bailey castles on either side of the current Welsh Border, marked by the River Ceiriog between Chirk and Weston Rhyn. The original Quinta estate was partly bounded by Offa's Dyke built along the Anglo-Welsh border by Offa, King of Mercia, probably during the 780s. Watt's Dyke, constructed some 80 years earlier, runs 40 miles through the northern Welsh Marshes and within the eastern part of the Quinta three-mile circle.

LOCATIONS

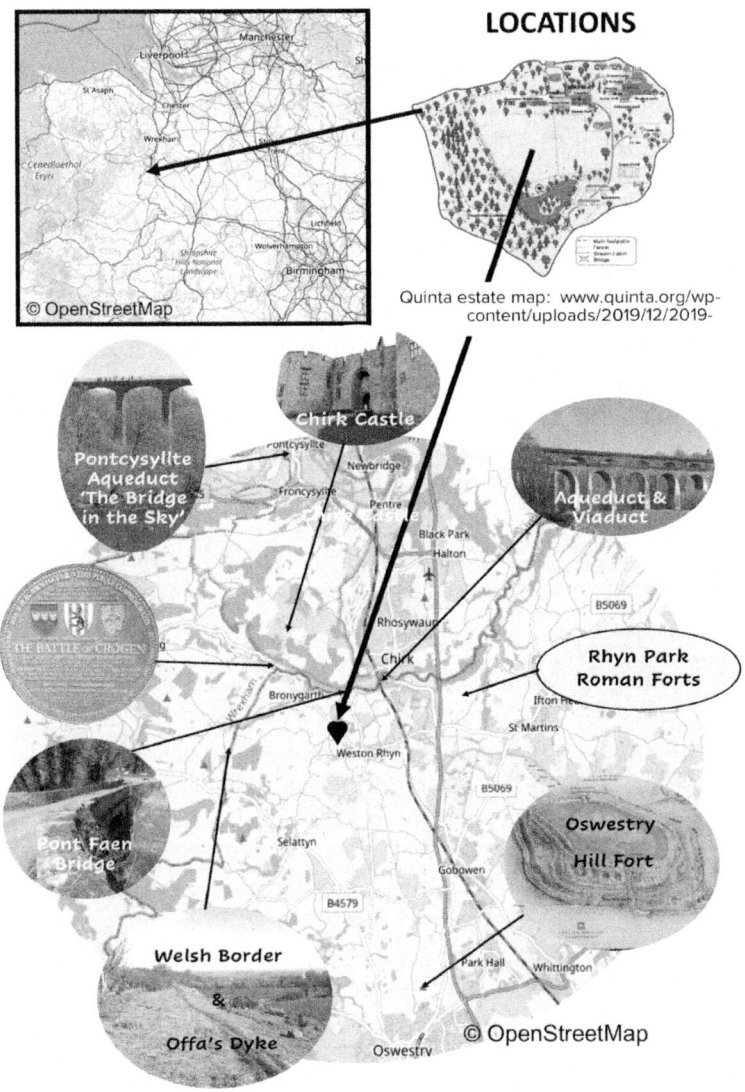

Quinta estate map: www.quinta.org/wp-content/uploads/2019/12/2019-

In the eleventh century, Weston Rhyn is recorded as "Westune" in the 'Doomsday Book' of 1086. The Quinta once owned a considerable part of Weston Rhyn. On the northwest corner of the former estate is the site of the Battle of Crogen. Here, in 1165, Owain Gwynedd successfully held back the army of King Henry II, who was mounting a campaign against an alliance of Welsh princedoms. Many soldiers on both sides were killed. Near the site is a veteran oak, now badly split but thought to be over 1,200 years old. Known as the "Oak at the Gate of the Dead", it reputedly marks the mass burial ground from the battle. Later, the campaign was abandoned after an attempt to cross the Berwyn Mountains was thwarted by severe weather. However, Henry had murdered hostages and burned villages, including churches. Owain's sons wanted to attack English churches in revenge, but Owain said it was vital to have God on their side.

Gerald of Wales regarded the English defeat at Crogen as a lesson from God. Two decades later, he referred to the battle in the description of his tour of Wales in 1188. He wrote that the area was noted for its stud farms, breeding fine horses of Spanish ancestry.[5] I mention this as an entirely new and speculative version of the same theory: that Spanish connections created the name "The Quinta" but at a time much earlier than is currently thought. Border tensions remained. Chirk Castle, built in 1295 to the north on the opposite side of the River Ceiriog, was another former estate boundary of The Quinta.

The Castle was part of King Edward I's chain of fortresses across northern Wales, guarding the entrance to the Ceiriog Valley.

Finally, some 2,700 years after the hill fort was started, a new army camp was created during the First World War. Park Hall Camp was capable of housing 21,000 soldiers. It was used again in the Second World War to train volunteers and conscripts. It was closed in 1975 after being used to train men on National Service. Altogether, well over 50,000 soldiers will have been trained at Park Hall. So, far from being only part of a remote country idyll, The Quinta is closely surrounded by an extensive archaeological chronology. 3,000 years of our military history, dating back to around 800 BC. It is not surprising that many examples of transport history are found in "The Quinta three-mile circle."

From ancient times, as livestock were moved to market or between winter and summer pastures, they would be driven through the locality of The Quinta. With the Roman fort nearby, there were road connections to the Roman cities of Chester and Wroxeter (Virconium Cornoviorum), one of the largest cities in Roman Britain. It is just over five miles southeast of Shrewsbury. The Romans would also have built roads to take them up the valleys and over the hills from their camp into Wales. For example, Weston Rhyn has an interesting Welsh street name: "Palmantmawr", which local historian Mark explains as meaning "The Great Footpath". Apparently, some flat stones were discovered during nearby roadworks in the late 1960s. Mark also suggests that "Quintana", in Latin, means a road between two camps and invites people to draw their own conclusions.

The ancient London to Holyhead coaching route, which borders the east of the former estate, is now part of the old London to Holyhead route. The 1675 Ogilby strip road map of the route from Chester to Cardiff shows it passing over Pont Faen Bridge, known to have existed since the fifteenth century, and the former Quinta Estate before proceeding to Selattyn. The Lodge public house, located in the centre of Weston Rhyn at the five-way junction, is believed to be a former coaching inn. Following this line of thinking, it becomes teasingly plausible to suggest that the name "The Quinta" dates back to Roman times, as it could have been the meeting point of five roads.

Llangollen Canal was built on the boundary of The Quinta estate around 1800, and the nearby Chirk Aqueduct was completed in 1801. The canal served the estate's coal mine, brickworks, quarries and lime kilns. A horse-drawn railway connected the canal to the estate offices and workshops near Quinta Hall. Evidence shows that these included a small sawmill, a smithy and a gasworks.

The more famous Pontcysyllte Aqueduct is three miles further north. It was referred to as Thomas Telford's "Bridge in the Sky" and was completed four years later in 1805. Were a feather in the cap of our three-mile Quinta circle required, it would be difficult to beat the fact that the stretch of canal from The Quinta to

Llangollen is now the "Pontcysyllte Aqueduct & Canal World Heritage Site".

The railways were to follow with a station in Weston Rhyn. The new Shrewsbury to Wrexham line was completed in 1848. This connected with the North Wales Mineral line and created the Shrewsbury to Chester line. This line was also connected from Gobowen to Oswestry, which became the headquarters of the Cambrian Railways.

Whilst the name "The Quinta" is uncommon in the UK, there is at least one other in England. In 1948, the well-known astronomer Sir Bernard Lovell bought The Quinta near Congleton. That private house remains today. Lovell planted an arboretum, which now covers 28 acres. It is known as the Lovell Quinta Arboretum and is open to the public daily.

Another theory suggests that the name "Quinta" indicates that the land was the fifth inherited share of a large estate. Again, this is a plausible explanation, but no evidence supports this theory. The grains of truth in all these theories are enough to tease. It is not easy to dismiss any theory entirely. A mystery is left. The origin of the name is uncertain. Those who are comfortable with uncertainty will enjoy this. Others who need to tie every detail down will be less comfortable.

THE WILD WEST SHOW

From 1800, records about The Quinta gradually become more available, but even these facts have blurred edges.

As you discover the time when The Quinta belonged to the landed aristocracy, you are invited to spot the famous names on the fringes of The Quinta story.

QUINTA TIMELINE circa 1800 1850

Chapter 2
The Wild West Show: Land, Wealth and Power

It is not known when Frederick West or his family bought The Quinta. But after 1800, records started to reveal that he was the owner. Before explaining who Frederick was, I must clarify a common confusion. The proliferation of Frederick Wests makes the story difficult to follow.

Frederick West himself, 1767-1852
Frederick's son: Frederick Richard West, 1799-1862
Frederick's grandsons: Frederick Myddelton West, 1831-1868
William Cornwallis West, 1835-1917
Frederick's great-grandson: George Frederick Myddelton West, 1874-1951

To avoid confusion, I will refer to Frederick Richard West simply as "Richard". Frederick's grandson, William, later changed his surname from "West" to "Cornwallis-West."

Frederick West belonged to an aristocratic landowning family with a history going back to the thirteenth century. The family estates in Hampshire were traditionally inherited by the oldest surviving male heir. Among Frederick's ancestors were influential courtiers in the reigns of Henry VIII and Elizabeth I.

Thomas West, the 12th Lord De La Warr, was commissioned Governor of Virginia in 1610. The USA state of Delaware was named after the Delaware River, which derived its name from Lord De La Warr when Europeans first explored the river.

Frederick West was the ninth of ten children. His father was a lieutenant general. Frederick was educated at Harrow School. The destiny of the children who were not heirs frequently lay in the marriage market. The interconnections of these families were endless. Land owned by men was the key to wealth and power. A "good marriage" was essential to maintaining a place in society. A seat in Parliament often came hand in hand with property ownership. Although Frederick lived to the ripe old age of 85, his third oldest brother lived long enough to provide an heir to the De La Warr estates.

So, Frederick's destiny lay elsewhere. His first wife died early. In 1798, at the age of 31, he married Maria Myddelton. The Myddelton family had occupied Chirk Castle from 1595 and owned extensive estates in North Wales. Richard Myddelton, like his father, was a Member of Parliament for Denbigh Boroughs. He died unmarried in 1796. The estate was left to his two sisters, Charlotte and Maria and half-sister Harriet. It is reported that when Frederick West married Maria, he took up residence at Chirk Castle. Three years later, he was elected as the MP for Denbighshire Burroughs.

However, in 1801, Maria's older sister, Charlotte, married Robert Biddulph, an MP from Herefordshire.

They also lived at the Castle. In 1802, Robert lost his Herefordshire Parliamentary seat, and a lengthy and acrimonious legal dispute developed over the inheritance. It had political overtones because Frederick had to surrender his seat in Parliament to Robert Biddulph. This expensive litigation lasted about two decades and was eventually settled by an Act of Parliament. The estate was divided into three portions.

Harriet, the third sister, inherited Ruthin Castle. She was the only child of her father's second marriage and was close to her half-sister, Maria. Harriet decided to build a large house on top of the medieval castle ruins at Ruthin Castle. This became the centre of the combined Maria and Harriet portions of the former Chirk Castle estate. Frederick West became involved in running the Ruthin estate. Harriet did not marry and bequeathed the estate to Maria's family on her death in 1848. On Frederick's death, a few years after Harriett, Richard inherited the Ruthin estate from Harriett and the Llanarmon Dyffryn Ceiriog estate from his mother.[6]

So, the role of The Quinta in their lives is far from clear. Even in normal circumstances, landed families like theirs often resided in several different houses throughout the year. These usually included a base in London. Sometimes, where they lived was linked to events or the time of year. Sometimes, they also spent significant periods abroad. It is not known how much time they spent at The Quinta. It is reasonable to believe that Frederick would have used The Quinta for some of the time up to 1826, when he and

Maria were probably not welcome at Chirk Castle, and while they were waiting for the outcome of the inheritance issues. However, there are records of them also living in Hampshire. King George III visited Frederick there in 1804.[7]

When the early rebuilding at Ruthin was complete, it would seem logical that the family spent most of their time between Ruthin, Hampshire and London but not at The Quinta. All that is known for certain is that The Quinta was owned by Frederick West and was not sold until 1852, the year of Frederick's death. At times, it was rented out.

Despite this uncertainty about The Quinta's role, improvements were made to The Quinta estate. A mock Stonehenge was built. Accounts provide different dates for this, ranging from 1830 to 1840. Some attribute this work to Frederick, while others attribute it to his son, Richard. Frederick and Maria may have been helping to finance Ruthin Castle, so it is unclear why they would have been interested in developing The Quinta. Perhaps it could have been for their son, Richard, if The Quinta was seen as his primary English residence. The mock Stonehenge stone has visible quarry drilling holes. It is known that the family had industrial interests in mining and quarrying at Llanymynech, Ruabon and Wrexham.[7]

Richard West married Theresa Cornwallis-Whitby in 1827, extending the families' extensive connections. Theresa's grandfather was Admiral Sir William Cornwallis, a friend and contemporary of Nelson. Her father, John Whitby, was also a notable naval officer. Richard and Theresa lived abroad in Florence for several years, where some of their children were born. It is not clear whether they spent any time at The Quinta. Richard and Theresa were interested in art.[8] Also, the fact that his father was well-established at Ruthin suggests that Richard and Theresa may have had a hand in creating the mock Stonehenge.

As well as the mock Stonehenge, two curious tunnels, seemingly in the middle of nowhere on the estate, are still used today as part of public footpaths. It is said that bridleways were created on the estate for family members to use when riding. Where these crossed public footpaths, a tunnel was made for the footpaths to go underneath the rides so that the family did not have to mix with the local people.

When her mother died in 1850, Theresa took over the running of Newlands Manor in Hampshire, where she would return from Ruthin to live in a reclusive style after her husband Richard died in 1868. Newlands was to play an even more significant part in their children's lives than Ruthin. In 1848, Richard, then 63 years old, commissioned further rebuilding and extensions at Ruthin while his father was still alive. The Quinta was clearly becoming surplus to the family's requirements. When Frederick died in 1852, The Quinta was sold to Thomas Barnes.

To conclude this part of the journey through The Quinta story, I will share briefly the headlines of what happened to the West family afterwards. This includes one of the greatest scandals of the period. In most of what follows, I am indebted to the work of Raymond Curry on the story of the Cornwallis-West Family. He provides considerably more detail.[7]

Richard West died in 1862, only 10 years after his father. For his son, William Cornwallis-West, the death of his father was a significant turning point in his life. He, too, had been living a relaxed lifestyle in Florence, where he was born. Not quite 30 years old, William returned to Ruthin to assume the responsibilities of a country landowner, holding roles such as Lord Lieutenant of Denbighshire and the local Member of Parliament. Apparently, he left his children behind in Florence, but he was still unmarried.

It was his marriage that cemented William's name in history. He married Mary Fitzpatrick. She was known as Patsy all her life. Patsy's mother, Olivia, whose father was Lord Chamberlain to the Queen, had been banished back to Ireland from court in London because she allegedly tried to seduce Queen Victoria's husband, Prince Albert. Much later, Olivia and Patsy returned to England and became part of the Edward, Prince of Wales, set. Both mother and daughter were renowned for their beauty and charm. It was not long before Patsy gained the attention of the promiscuous Edward, Prince of Wales. They fell in love and had a long-term relationship.

To facilitate this relationship with Prince Edward, Patsy needed to marry. William Cornwallis-West became captivated by Patsy. He married Patsy in October 1872, despite this being against his mother's wishes and the reality that Patsy was only 16 and 19 years younger and was widely known to be in a relationship with Prince Edward.

They had three children. Daisy married a German Prince, and Shelagh married the Duke of Westminster. Their son, George Frederick Myddelton West, married Jennie Jerome (Lady Randolph Churchill), the mother of Winston Churchill. After their divorce, George married a renowned actress.[9]

At the turn of the century, the West family, especially Patsy, remained part of high society and led a notoriously decadent lifestyle, to the extent that the Prince of Wales referred to them as "The Wild West Show". Mainly at Newlands in Hampshire, but also at Ruthin Castle, there were parties and many social gatherings that included people of the highest influence in the land: from society, politics and the military establishment. One of Patsy's favourite party tricks was to toboggan down Ruthin Castle stairs on a tea tray in the presence of the future king.[10] Patsy's relationship with Edward did not last. There was a scandal too far. Patsy fell from influence and died in 1920, three years after William. William's financial arrangements were weak, and his son George was a spendthrift.

A Bronygarth family living close to The Quinta has a handwritten copy of William Cornwallis-West's last will and testament, dated 1892.[11] It is a sad story. He tries to ensure his wife can continue living at Newlands Manor rent-free. He leaves to his heir all his real estate, if any, and the residue of his personal effects, subject to the payment of all his debts, for the use of and repair of Ruthin Castle.

It is unsurprising that, upon William's death in 1917, Ruthin Castle was sold to settle debts. Shelagh was later divorced, ending the West's connection with the wealthy Westminster family. George died by his own hand in 1951 while suffering from Parkinson's disease. So, despite making headlines around the turn of the century, the Cornwallis-West family, along with many other landed families, faded from view in the wake of the First World War. Their time was over. Whilst they made their mark in society and history, they left no lasting social heritage.

The West's departure in 1852 heralded a completely different era for The Quinta. Intriguingly, a Myddelton heir would briefly become involved with The Quinta Story well over 100 years later.

PETER BEVINGTON

AN INSPIRATIONAL LIFE

The West dynasty is replaced by another. Their home is demolished.

Thomas Barnes, the new owner of The Quinta makes big changes and leaves a heritage that is worth celebrating.

Individuals can make a difference.

Quinta Hall c 1900

QUINTA TIMELINE 1850 1900

Chapter 3
An Inspirational Life

Note

I was taken on this part of the journey through The Quinta story by Jennifer Barnes. Jennifer appeared in my office in Quinta Hall in 2006. She was researching Thomas Barnes, but she soon realised she was unrelated. However, she was so enthralled by her discoveries that she devoted many years to meticulous research, which informs this part of the journey through the history of The Quinta. With her permission, only the more significant elements of her work are referenced.[12]

Humble Beginnings Ride the Wave of the Industrial Revolution

In the village of Farnworth, on the moors near Bolton, approximately 10 miles northwest of Manchester, Thomas Barnes was born in 1812, just six years before the birth of Queen Victoria. As his life began, the Industrial Revolution brought significant change to the region. It would not be until Thomas was 40 years old that he purchased The Quinta.

To understand Thomas, we need to appreciate his upbringing and background. In contrast to the West family, he was from a hardworking family. His father,

James Rothwell Barnes, was an entrepreneur. James began a cottage industry, handing out warp and weft to home-based handloom weavers. James built a weaving shed two years before Thomas was born, but it was not until later that James introduced Farnworth's first steam-powered mill in 1828. He was a close associate of Thomas Bonsor Crompton, a local paper mill owner. Together, they are regarded as the founding fathers of Farnworth. They brought the full impact of the Industrial Revolution to the town. By 1832, James had expanded to include cotton spinning.

Thomas' family began as ordinary working people. Thomas knew what hard work was and how the poorest lived: just an accident or illness away from deprivation. Thomas' family were also involved in education. In 1838, along with other mill owners, they established a school to provide basic education for the children of their workers. Through hard work and innovation, his father laid the foundations which enabled Thomas to become rich and influential. Their attitudes were carved out in a demanding working-class environment.

His father and others were active in their Christian faith and worked for the benefit of local churches. Thomas left school at 14 years old to help his brother, George, manage their father's business, as their father was ill. Thomas' early ambition was to become a minister in the Congregational Church. He began teaching in Sunday School at the age of 18.

He worked his way up to become Superintendent till he withdrew from this role in 1851. He also became one of four deacons at the Chapel at Halshaw Moor. He was elected to the Committee of the Bible Society and regularly supported the London Missionary Society, of which he had become a director by 1864.

As we uncover a few more of the many causes that Thomas became involved in, it is worth remembering his overriding commitment to his local Chapel. Three times, or at least twice, every Sunday for 30 years, he would serve at the Chapel. While still working alongside his brother George, running the family business, he may have held on to his ambition to become a minister until he was in his thirties. His father's persuasion and circumstances led him to settle for a life as a businessman. However, he may also have gradually become aware of other opportunities to serve through business and politics.

Thomas' life was never far from tragedy. Of his five siblings, only Thomas and his older sister, Jane, lived to old age. His younger sisters, Mary, died at 22 and Sarah at 16. His younger brother, James, died aged 21 in an accident at one of their mills. Thomes had married Sarah Richardson, daughter of another cotton mill owner, in 1834. Their first child died aged just five weeks in October 1835, and his wife died a few months later in December. Within a year, Thomas married his deceased wife's sister, Ann. His older brother George, who had been carrying the main weight of running the business, died about a decade later in 1844. This left Thomas to take over. Thomas' parents both died five or so years later, having buried four of their six children. So, when he was 38, Thomas had sole ownership of a very successful business. He had also inherited £30,000. He expanded the company and took on partners. It became a prominent cotton manufacturing company with a key role in Lancashire's economic growth.

Thomas had already diversified. He was heavily involved with railways to the extent that he eventually became Chairman of the Lancashire and Yorkshire Railway Company, one of the largest rail networks of its time. This interest in railways was international: he had stakes in at least two railway companies abroad. His other business interests were extensive. He was a director of the Bank of Bolton and Chairman of the Provincial Insurance Company based in Wrexham. He contributed to the energy sector through the Farnworth and Kearsley Gas Company and invested in Welsh slate quarries. Like many others, he drove and rode the fruit of the Industrial Revolution. Their horizons stretched far beyond England. The world was opening up, and investments and influence paid rich dividends as engineering and construction took off in Britain and across the globe. Despite this, there were ups and downs and times when, like many entrepreneurs, Thomas suffered heavy financial losses. Thomas had another interest. In the 1840s, he won prizes at Farnworth Agricultural Shows; however, it was not until his time at The Quinta that his passion for agriculture and horticulture became fully established.

At the beginning of 1851, Thomas had a serious

accident. He was travelling in a small horse carriage with his groom on Moor Lane, Bolton. For some reason, the horse took fright. They collided with a coal cart. His groom was thrown. While Thomas tried to grab the reins, he collided with a lamp post. Thomas was also thrown, but his leg got caught in the spokes of a moving wheel. He had to have his foot amputated. But this would not slow Thomas down. In fact, reading about his entire life, it is easy to forget that for much of his adult life, he was disabled.

Politically Engaged

Thomas began to get involved politically in the late 1830s. At 40, he was elected MP for Bolton in 1852. He lost the election in 1857 but returned to Parliament in 1861 for another seven years.

His speech to his electorate in 1852 reveals a list of the causes he was determined to support.[13] These included free trade and the controversial debate regarding the Corn Laws, which Thomas strongly opposed. The Corn Laws were tariffs and trade restrictions on imported grain designed to protect farmers by keeping grain prices high. They benefited landowners but increased food prices for the general population. He was also keen on parliamentary reform, advocating the extension of the franchise to every property owner and wanting proper ballots to be part of the Reform Bill.

He was highly critical of the unequal distribution of parliamentary seats. He gave the example of Middlesex, which had 242,798 inhabited houses compared to Dorset's 34,771. These two counties each elected an equal number of Members of Parliament. He had much to say about taxation and spending. He advocated for direct taxation, citing a tax on soap as unhelpful, given the need for public hygiene. He criticised inefficient naval spending: "Ships built that cannot sail, some that turn up like a dead fish on one side, some floating in the dock for a very short time and then pronounced unseaworthy." Similarly, he decried army spending promoted by foolish talk about a French invasion. He criticised unnecessary deployments of troops across the Empire.

Thomas wanted to separate state and religion, arguing that the government should leave all religions alone. He supported freedom of expression and opposed any grants to religious groups. Despite a heavy commitment and generous donations to the school founded by his father in 1885, Thomas opposed state education because it primarily benefited middle-class children rather than those from poorer backgrounds. He concluded his speech by saying, "It is the purpose of my life to do everything I can, in every possible way, to elevate myself and those around me on the scale of morality. It is righteousness that exalts a nation, and sin is a reproach to any people."

Thomas' political career was not without its challenges. At times, Thomas' views differed from those of his colleagues. After he lost the 1857 election, when some wanted him to stand as an MP for Bury, he commented: "I am not radical enough for Bolton, and too radical for Bury, so between the two stools I fall." Politics was not the easiest of arenas for a man of strong principles. Conflict was inherent in politics. Possibly as part of a broader issue, Thomas' first election was beset by allegations of bribery and corruption during the election. These were eventually dismissed as frivolous and vexatious.

One of the main issues of his time was the fight against slavery. As a cotton magnate, he was deeply involved on all fronts. He was a vocal opponent of slavery. His actions spoke louder than words. For some time, as an extension of his cotton manufacturing business, he and others had been interested in expanding their involvement in diversifying the global cotton supply.

The situation became urgent due to the American Civil War (1861–65), which completely disrupted the cotton supply to Europe, leading to the Lancashire Cotton Famine. Cotton stocks ran out towards the end of 1861. The following year, 1862, was dire for the Manchester area. Mill closures, mass unemployment and poverty struck northern Britain. There were ugly sides to this problem, with some merchants selling cotton stocks back to America for higher prices and some owners distancing themselves from helping their redundant employees.

Several riots occurred in Manchester and its surrounding areas in 1863. However, it appears that Bolton suffered a little less, perhaps due to the efforts of Thomas and his friends. He was well-known for his rapport with his workers by hosting popular events such as New Year's parties. He agreed at one time to reduce the working day from twelve hours to eleven hours without loss of pay. Apparently, other owners followed his example.

Thomas was deeply involved in the cotton famine issue as a local mill owner, a respected local philanthropist and a politician. In Parliament, he made very clear his opposition to the Southern states in the United States of America: "Nothing will induce me to acknowledge slavery or the right to maintain slaves."

He was involved in attempts to grow cotton in India. Unfortunately, one attempt ended with expensive machines rusting away on a beach. In 1862, Thomas purchased a 200-acre cotton plantation in Jamaica. He wanted to show that cotton could be produced profitably without exploiting slave labour. He was amongst the first, if not the first, to offer cash wages and prove the viability of ethical production. Within a year, 210 acres were successfully cultivated, making his plantation a model of sustainability. However, these and other efforts were not without problems. On the back of his success in employing former slaves, he demonstrated that good work could be achieved when people were paid fairly. He even showed that it was cheaper overall to employ people than to keep a slave.

Thomas spoke vigorously in Parliament against the then widely proposed suggestion that Black people were inferior and lazy. He was openly opposed to the racist attitudes of the nineteenth century.

Thomas and his colleagues fought against the prejudices and injustices of their time on multiple fronts, both nationally and internationally. Having spent time in New Zealand and learned about the Treaty of Waitangi, I was intrigued to discover that Thomas was a signatory to a letter to The Times supporting the cause of the Māori people in New Zealand. With his nephew Alfred, he toured Ireland to research the problems there.

This brief journey has only scratched the surface, uncovering the headlines. There is much more to tell about this man who purchased The Quinta Estate from the West Family in 1852. It is interesting to reflect that in our time, many families and organisations are engaging in soul-searching remorse regarding their ancestors' or benefactors' entanglement in profiteering from the slave trade. Thomas Barnes was a champion in these matters, a long way ahead of his time. He is a part of Quinta's heritage that can be celebrated with pride.

The Move to The Quinta

The obvious question is, why did Thomas buy The Quinta? Why did he not stick with his egalitarian principles and remain in a modest house in Farnworth? Thomas and his colleagues were pioneering a new social order, but echoes of the past remained.

Power and influence were beginning to transition from the landed aristocracy. The old brand of politician was the foremost landowner in the area. The new brand of politician was the foremost businessman.

Unsurprisingly, the new rich emulated traditional landed families like the West family. Some built substantial mansions. They sought election to Parliament as the means to change the status quo. Like those they were replacing, they often resided in multiple residences throughout the year. They also tended to intermarry within their own tight social circles. Both Thomas and his son married daughters of other mill owners. Quinta Hall was small compared to many new Victorian country-house projects of the mid-nineteenth century. When it was sold in 1934, the Sale Catalogue listed four reception rooms, a billiard room, a conservatory, thirteen bed and dressing rooms, four bathrooms and a domestic quarter. In a later speech, Thomas revealed that one of his reasons for coming to The Quinta was "...that he might be able to give his ministerial friends an opportunity for pleasant and profitable relaxation when, by overwork, they had become exhausted and needed rest." This would account for more bedrooms than the family needed.

When Thomas purchased the Quinta, the 3,300-acre estate included numerous farms and woodlands. He probably wanted to fulfil his lifelong interest in agriculture and horticulture. The Quinta gardens, conservatories and greenhouses were to serve as engine houses for the numerous shows at The Quinta and in the surrounding locality. The grounds would be used for hospitality for thousands. The benefit for his wife's health might have been another reason for a move to the country. Thomas was to spend his time between Farnworth, Westminster and The Quinta, where he sought to develop a model Victorian estate that reflected his principles and values.

Thomas had moved to The Quinta by 1855. Initially, the family lived in a house on the estate. He demolished the original Quinta residence and built a new Victorian-style house using the stone from the original building. He moved into the new Quinta Hall in 1856. Whilst Quinta Hall was being built, he began a renovation programme for his estate properties to benefit his tenants.

His attitude is reflected in an entry in one of his diaries. "Money is a difficult thing; it is hard to get and hard to keep and troublesome to manage well. I ought not to be covetous or filled with the cares of this world. I ought, as a matter of duty, to look after and take care of such property as God gives me. I ought to look on it as an instrument of usefulness". This diary entry demonstrates a mindset that would profoundly influence the heritage of The Quinta. It is strikingly different from the mindset behind most country estates. Thomas set a pattern that his family would follow. It would also characterise the future of The Quinta as it unfolded over the following 150 years.

An immediate priority for Thomas was to build a church. It took only four months and was opened in October 1858. The Quinta Church was built at the bottom of the drive close to the main village, which was then known as The Lodge before it became Weston Rhyn. Many churches on country estates are deliberately built next to the main mansion and are primarily for the family. This was not his church but a church for the local people.

Twenty-five years later, Thomas built the Quinta Sunday School. There is a detailed account of the cost of this building, which amounted to a total of £3,405.4s.8d. The 46,500 Ruabon bricks used cost £46.8s.[14] Approximately a third of the cost was covered by the Sunday School's own resources, fundraising and public subscription. The rest was given by Thomas Barnes, his family and friends. No expense was spared. The building was deliberately elaborate and finished to a high standard because Thomas and the family wanted this to be a memorial to his second wife, Ann. The designer was Thomas Raffles Davison, a famous architect who happened to be the son of a man who became the minister of Quinta Church. It was opened in 1883.

From the outset, Thomas steadily developed the estate's infrastructure. The stables and the workshops were rebuilt and developed. That area would eventually contain estate offices, some accommodation for estate workers, carriages and carts and stables for horses.

There were also workshops, a timber yard, a smithy and even a gasworks. Eventually, these were connected by a horse-drawn railway track to the canal and the Quinta Colliery and Brick Works.

Later, a fire engine was housed there. Folklore has it that, on one occasion, a house in the village burnt to the ground because it took so long to catch the horse in the neighbouring field. Quinta Hall was built in the Gothic Victorian style, heavily influenced by Augustus Pugin, one of the architects involved with the design of the Houses of Parliament in London. Pugin is reputed to have designed some of the furniture. The style was not to everyone's taste. Many local people were critical of the style. A descendant of Thomas' brother George described it as "a somewhat forbidding Victorian house".[15] However, Thomas and his family made it into a lavishly decorated home furnished in the style of the time. As we will discover later, Quinta Hall underwent savage architectural desecration in the twentieth century. So, apart from the overall impact of the Victorian exterior, only a few hints remain of what was: carvings of texts on the outside of the building and a handful of remnants inside. This includes the fireplace, which still dominates the entrance hall.

The Quinta was a centre of hospitality from early in the Barnes era. Even before the new building was finished, there were visits from local people, including Sunday School children. In 1859, Thomas invited his fellow Liberals from Bolton, Bury and Farnworth for a day out.

A special, inexpensive railway excursion was laid on to Chirk Station for 1,000 guests, departing from Bury at 6 am and arriving just after 11 am. Tents with seats and tables had been erected, and refreshments were provided before the usual speeches. Having recently lost his seat, Thomas quipped, "He was more inclined to have a seat in the country than in Parliament."

In 1860, four to five hundred of Thomas' employees from Farnworth travelled to The Quinta for the day, and the band of the Farnworth Rifle Corps accompanied them. Thomas' son, James, was the band's musical director. On this occasion, they were joined by many local people, once again making about 1,000 visitors. It rained all day, but a large canvas-covered shed had been put up to accommodate the activities and refreshments. These events present a remarkable pen picture of The Quinta, where Thomas Barnes bought new life. In all aspects of his life, whether in Farnworth, Quinta, or Westminster, Thomas was an outstanding representative of a new generation of leaders. Collectively, they had a profound impact on the politics of Britain, the Empire and consequently, the world. They were individuals who made a difference.

The journey now shifts its focus to Thomas' daughter-in-law, Ellen. She would put many of Thomas' aspirations and values into practice at The Quinta before his death in 1897. Therefore, Thomas' influence on The Quinta journey, whilst largely hidden, is not yet over.

PETER BEVINGTON

A REMARKABLE WOMAN

Ellen Barnes' contribution to The Quinta heritage overlaps with that of her father-in-law, Thomas.

She makes an impact on the local community, especially on the lives of children and young people.

An event in 1871 gives an insight into The Quinta in its Victorian splendour.

Bronygarth School

Ellen Barnes

Tile Mural, Quinta Sunday Schools

QUINTA TIMELINE 1860 1920

Chapter 4
A Remarkable Woman

Introduction

Until a few years ago, Ellen Barnes had just been a name to me, even though I had been connected to The Quinta for nearly half a century and was a Trustee of her Charity, The Ellen Barnes Charitable Trust. When the Trust decided to research its 100 year history, an archive box was rediscovered, gathering dust in the solicitor's basement. Inside was a large leather-bound book. On the first two pages, with an elaborately illuminated heading, was a handwritten biography of Ellen Barnes.[16] Then, out of the blue, Jennifer Barnes contacted The Quinta, wanting to pass on material about Ellen Barnes. I ended up with a copy of her unpublished 60 page chronicle of the life of Ellen and her husband, Thomas Barnes' son, James Richardson Barnes. So, again, I owe her credit for much of my material.[17]

Another Christian Lancashire Mill Family

Ellen Barnes [nee Cheetham] was born in 1842 into a prosperous cotton manufacturing family in Stalybridge founded by her grandfather, George Cheetham. Her father, John Cheetham, and her brother, John Fredrick Cheetham, were Liberal MPs. The family attended Stalybridge Congregational

Church. Ellen married into an almost identical family. With their origins in Farnworth and Stalybridge on either side of Manchester, the two families shared extensive faith, political and business interests. Both families were heavily involved in the Liberal Party. Thomas Barnes was elected MP for Bolton on three occasions between 1852 and 1869. Ellen's father was MP for South Lancashire from 1852 to 1857. Her brother was an MP for North Derbyshire from 1880 to 1885 and Stalybridge from 1906 to 1910.

Faith, politics and business all aligned for both families, as evidenced by their genuine interest in their communities. John and Thomas' worlds would have overlapped significantly in Manchester and Westminster. They would be well-acquainted with William Gladstone and many leading figures of this great era in British history. Thomas Barnes and John Cheetham both established Congregational Sunday Schools and provided substantial resources to local public services. Both were the benefactors behind public parks that still exist in Farnworth and Stalybridge.

It would be a mistake to view these families as merely dour, driven Victorian Protestants; they knew how to celebrate. When Ellen's future husband, James Richardson Barnes, came of age in 1860, Thomas celebrated by giving the local people Farnworth Park. They held a massive party.

The details are in this extract from 'The Farnworth of the Past' by H. Clare.[18]

"In the year 1860, Mr James Richardson Barnes, son of Mr Thomas Barnes, came of age at Quinta, Salop, and vast preparations were made to celebrate the event. A salute of 21 cannon notified Farnworth of the event, and the feasting began—32 rounds of beef, 200 pounds of sirloin, 30 legs of lamb, 28 hams, 30 tongues, 40 fowls, six turkeys, eight loads of potatoes, 600 pounds of plum pudding, 1,600 pounds of bread and 715 pounds of currant bread. This was for nearly 1,500 workpeople, their wives and invited guests. Dare I mention refreshment? ...20 dozen ginger beer, 20 dozen lemonade, 20 dozen cider, 250 gallons of beer, with 3,000 apples and 2,500 oranges. The feast took place in the mill. It was at this feast Mr Thomas Barnes handed over the gift of Farnworth Park to be forever the property of the people. The value of the gift at that time was estimated to be £11,000."

Ellen Barnes Enters The Quinta Story

The park was finally opened in 1864. The ceremony was delayed by almost three weeks to enable William Gladstone, Chancellor of the Exchequer, to give the main speech. Approximately 30,000 people assembled to see the procession. The next day, James Richardson Barnes married Ellen Cheetham. Jennifer Barnes discovered a lengthy report on the wedding from the Farnworth Observer on 15 October.

It was a big event in Stalybridge, with thousands of people lining the route to Melbourne Street Congregational Church. The Church was packed with almost a thousand people who were present two hours before the service. The bride, Ellen, is described as "...looking extremely beautiful in a white, corded silk dress with flounces of Honiton lace and a very elegant Brussels lace fall covering her from head to foot, adorned with a wreath of orange blossoms and jessamine." Meanwhile, in Farnworth through the day, there was continued firing of cannons at the cotton mills, and the band also paraded.[17]

After a honeymoon on the Isle of Wight, James and Ellen lived briefly in the newly completed Quinta Manse, which would eventually be a home for the minister of the Quinta Church. When it was ready, they moved to Brookside in Bronygarth. Ellen was usually referred to as Mrs James Barnes, as was the custom of the time because her primary role was to be James' wife. James appears not to have been deeply involved in the cotton business or public life at Farnworth. Instead, he carved out a life in and around The Quinta and Denbighshire.

James was clearly involved with running The Quinta Estate as early as 1871 when the Census described him as a landowner. As evidenced by his will, James owned the estate by 1885, despite his father's residence at Quinta Hall.

He followed the family's political allegiances and was involved in Liberal events in Shropshire and Denbighshire.

James and Ellen's faith underpinned their lives, just as it did for other family members. They were influential long-term members of the Quinta Church. From its opening in 1858, the Quinta Church was a central element in the lives of the Barnes family and those close to them in the locality. Ellen and James are buried outside the Church. However, the Ellen Barnes Charitable Trust record book states that: "Her sympathies were not confined to her own denomination, and she was a liberal supporter of all religious and philanthropic organisations in the area." [19]

Much later, in 1883, because her father-in-law, Thomas Barnes was ill, Ellen opened the Sunday School building. It was just down the road from the Church. For this, she was given a memento: a silver key. Her husband, James, was passionate about music from an early age. His father bought him a concertina when he was 15. Ellen shared his love of music. Occasionally, they performed together. Ellen was a notable pianist. They combined their music with their faith. James became the choirmaster at the Quinta Church, and Ellen became the organist. They were top of the bill in the grand concert, which marked the opening of the Quinta Sunday Schools building in 1883. This listed building is sadly underused today, but in Ellen's time, it was a vibrant element in community life, with concerts, shows and other events held there in addition to its primary function.

At one time, the Sunday School had an attendance of about 300, including nearly 80 infants. In addition to all her other commitments, Ellen led a girls' class in the Sunday School until a few years before her death. This 35 year commitment is a remarkable echo of her father-in-law's commitment to Sunday School teaching in Farnworth.

Apart from supporting, accompanying, and sometimes deputising for his father in various meetings and events, James was a Denbighshire magistrate from 1868 and remained active in the 1890s. He was one of the 48 people elected to the new Denbigh County Council — in fact, he was second in the election, with only one vote behind the leader. In 1889, James served as a Justice of the Peace with commitments at the Quarter Sessions and Assizes. He was an Alderman of the Denbigh County Council. James exercised significant local leadership in contrast to his father's national and international concerns.

The Quinta in Its Victorian Splendour

Both James and Ellen were involved with Thomas in the life of this large country estate. From the early days of the new Quinta Hall, hundreds of visitors came to this relatively modest Victorian country home, in addition to a steady flow of individual guests.

Together, they made The Quinta "...a hospitable centre of non-conformist life in North Shropshire and the Welsh Borderland."[17] Although there had been many visits before, from 1870 onwards, the park and gardens were regularly used as a destination for Sunday School and Church trips.

A journalist reporting in The Oswestry Advertizer provides a glimpse of what The Quinta was like in its Victorian heyday.[20] In August 1871, Thomas opened the grounds of The Quinta and the ground floor of Quinta Hall for the Annual Oswestry Institute Fete and Picnic. Around three thousand people came. Many were brought by train to the station at Preesgweene. This article is possibly the most detailed account of The Quinta ever recorded. It provided a fascinating glimpse of Victorian country life:

"Mr Barnes threw open the lower suite of rooms. Both rooms and pleasure grounds were viewed by an almost endless stream of visitors. Although not a show house perhaps of the first order, there were many objects before which the lover of art would long linger, and which proved that the owner is a liberal patron of the Fine Arts. In the entrance hall, three large marble busts of Horace, Homer and Cobden on handsome pedestals were amongst the most noticeable objects, and visitors could not fail to be attracted by the handsome marble fireplace of the quaint mediaeval fashion above, which was a sculpture in old English characters of the old saying: "Warm ye in friendship".

In the breakfast room were hung some of the best-known works of Ansell and other English limners.

Lovers of the curious and rare in art had their curiosity gratified by a profuse display of proof engravings, which had an appropriate home in the well-stored library. The drawing room had several landscapes by Harding and John Phillips amongst its chief attractions. In the vestibule, Spencer's full-sized marble figure of Burns' "Highland Mary" attracted a large crowd of admirers.

The splendid, curved oak antique apportments (fixtures and fittings) of the dining room shared the general admiration which was bestowed upon the oil paintings which were hung in this room, the most notable of which was Goodall's "Last Load". The pictures were labelled with the names of the artists and the scenes or localities. This plan was greatly appreciated by the visitors and saved endless enquiries being made.

From the mansion, visitors passed through the billiard room into the conservatories, which were a perfect floral treasury. Most of the greenhouses were closed, but in the few that were open, the botanist could find abundant objects of study. If the passers-through possessed an eye only for the beautiful and a delicate perception of sweet perfumes, they were by no means unrewarded for their ramble through the tastefully laid-out grounds.

Tired of wandering through the house and grounds, numbers betook themselves to the terrace in front of the house, from which, the country stretching out for miles in front, they could admire the art and skill with which Mr Louden had drawn elaborate floral designs and beautified the grounds, how every shade of leaf had its appropriate contrast, and how every tint of flower, harmonising with its neighbour, fell in its proper place in the rich design. The arrangement of all this beauty is well rewarded by the result, and, if the admiration bestowed upon his labours may be any gratification to Mr Louden, he must be gratified in the highest degree.

It was a hot day with the thermometer at 80°F in the shade. The article went on to describe the activities outside, which included archery, croquet, quoits and skittles. There were leap bars, swings and gymnastic appliances of every kind. Races of 100 yards, 250 yards and a half-mile bicycle race were held. Balloons were set off at intervals during the afternoon; a troop, The Marionettes, exhibited and the band of the 15th Shropshire Rifle Volunteers played.

There were opportunities for dancing and an "Aunt Sally" with "An endless cloud of missiles flying all afternoon". Games in which forfeits occurred were the most popular, for forfeits meant kissing. The day ended with a trapeze artist performing on a high wire and fireworks."

Frequently, there would be other fetes, flower shows and gatherings at The Quinta, where family members both hosted and took significant roles, participating with their entries. Especially in the 1890s, there were reports of large marquees. Horticulture and agriculture were important elements of the shows. The Quinta Head Gardener, Mr. James Louden, was locally renowned, having often won awards or served as a Show Judge. Thomas and he won prizes for Quinta grapes at the RHS show in London. Garden parties and shows across the area must have taken up much of James and Ellen's time.

Ellen also became involved in an area event entitled "The Ceiriog Vale Industrial Art and Loan Exhibition" in the 1890s, held annually at Chirk Castle Park, Brynkinalt Park, or Quinta Park. The exhibition aimed "...to encourage those attending schools and young people generally in handicraft, art, etc." Ellen was one of the lady patronesses and an honorary secretary. This involved a lot of work. The second exhibition was held at The Quinta in 1892 and was a great success. The number of competitors increased to over 600, with a huge attendance. The entries were displayed at the Quinta Sunday School and a nearby field. The loan collection was displayed in Quinta Hall. It consisted of an art gallery and museum featuring a diverse and valuable collection of artefacts, some of which were sent from all over the country.

Ellen's Personal Impact

The life of The Quinta makes a delightful story, but in addition to all this, Ellen also carved out her personal interests. Ellen enjoyed the privileges of her class with a modest staff at Brookside. So, she could have had a very relaxed life as the local landowner's wife. Instead, she energetically expanded the interests of the Cheetham and Barnes families, making them her own. Her achievements would shape many people's lives and eventually extend beyond her death to future generations through her Trust.

Alongside the things already listed, education was a leading passion. Within a decade of Ellen's arrival, through the generosity of her father-in-law, the Bronygarth School was built and opened in Ellen's presence on 8 April 1872, with 18 girls. It was equipped in a style ahead of its time for an elementary school of its day.

Ellen was described as the lady manager. 'The Charity Record Book' claims that Mrs Barnes covered most of the school's maintenance costs until it was taken over by the Shropshire Education Authority in 1903. According to the 'School Records Book' held by the current owners of the Old School House, Bronygarth, Ellen visited the school almost every week for the first five years. This started five days after the school opened. On 12 April 1872, the teacher recorded Ellen's first visit and described giving a more advanced lesson on the cow. The teacher comments, "Almost without exception, the children are exceedingly backward and dull". Perhaps she had not yet begun to appreciate that her new pupils had more to offer than the purely academic.

In 1887, three cottages were built opposite the school: one for the Head Teacher, one for a teaching Assistant and one for the School Caretaker. This enabled the pupil numbers to rise from 100 to a remarkable 140.

When you consider Ellen's weekly commitments to the Sunday School and the Bronygarth School, along with the number of children involved, spanning around half a century, the extent of her influence over so many young lives suddenly comes to life. If nothing else, this was a remarkable achievement. Ellen's work for children and young people did not stop in Weston Rhyn and Bronygarth. She was also heavily involved in education in the area, serving as one of the first co-opted members of the Shropshire Education Authority and as one of the first governors of Llangollen County School.

Thomas had been a lifelong supporter of, and eventually, a Director of the London Missionary Society. Ellen continued this work. She was the first woman to be appointed a Director of the London Missionary Society. (LMS) This was one of the oldest British missionary societies. It was inter-denominational and evangelical. This was in line with both her faith and her politics. The LMS had connections to the movement for the abolition of slavery. David Livingstone, a missionary, explorer, and abolitionist, was an LMS missionary at one stage.

Ellen regularly attended meetings of this society and others till failing health precluded her from travelling. Little did she know that 65 years after her death, her home, The Quinta, would become the UK headquarters of one of the world's largest missions.

Shortly before Thomas Barnes died in 1897, Ellen and James moved to Quinta Hall. James, whose health had never been robust, died only two years later in 1899. So, Ellen became the owner of The Quinta Estate for 20 years.

No longer in her husband's shadow and already well respected, Ellen, 57, found herself owning a 3,300-acre, well-organised, modern Victorian estate. She owned over 40 farms and smallholdings, as well as more than 100 additional properties, which encompassed almost 600 acres of woodland. Add all this to her personal interests, and it is easy to see that her responsibilities were formidable.

A local person, whose family has a long history in the area, reports hearing that William Frith, Ellen's Agent, was widely regarded as "...one of the less charitable agents in the area." He was Ellen's enforcer and was responsible for this large estate. This would not have been easy, especially in wartime and with an ageing landlord. A century later, we cannot be sure precisely what Ellen was like to live and work with. Nor can we fully understand the dynamics of all the relationships within the estate's hierarchy.

What we do know is that Ellen's actions and her legacy demonstrate that she cared. She was not a remote landlord. She was involved with people at all levels.

Much later evidence from 1928 contradicts the hearsay about William Frith. He cared deeply about the estate and the locality. He even put his job on the line in a letter to Harold Barnes, who inherited The Quinta from Ellen, to ensure that the estate was not sold off to speculators and asset strippers but would be sold in such a way as to benefit the community.[21]

William Frith was also the Chair of a committee that raised funds to build the Weston Rhyn Institute. This work was led by Charles Price, who had returned to Weston Rhyn to retire in the place where he was born and grew up. He would have been well known to the Barnes family and possibly a product of their Sunday School work. He had provided £300 to buy the land for the Institute. Ellen, Charles and 13 other residents were the first Trustees of the charity that ran the Institute. Ellen and her sister each gave donations of £50. Ellen hosted a three-day bazaar in 1907 to raise money.

Jennifer Barnes described Ellen as "a woman to be reckoned with". Ellen had key roles in the Oswestry Division Liberal Executive and was twice President of the Oswestry Choral Society. 'The Charity Record Book' claims: "She took the greatest interest in the comfort and welfare of her tenants and was keen to carry out improvements on the estate. Many new cottages were built, and farmhouses were renovated.

A yearly garden party for the tenants became a "much hoped-for event".[22]

Ellen also maintained an influential philanthropic interest in Farnworth, providing land for a new Council school, an addition to the park and additional funds for the Congregational Churches. Ellen returned to Brookside around 1910. Failing health compelled her to withdraw from all public activity a few years before her death.

The First World War occurred in the concluding chapter of Ellen's life. She would have seen many of "her children" from the Bronygarth School, the Sunday Schools and her tenants go off to fight, and some never return. There would be much grief on the estate and many practical problems created by the brutality of the Great War.

Ellen died on 23 February 1920. She was buried alongside her husband in the grounds of The Quinta Church. On her instruction, her coffin was taken to the Church on one of the estate timber wagons. The cortege was led by an open carriage carrying all the flowers. Estate workers lined both sides of the road to the Church. The inscription on a memorial to Ellen in the Quinta Church reads, "A devoted and liberal helper in every good work."

DEATH AND THE SEEDS OF LIFE

Ellen Barnes died childless. There was no direct heir. An era ended.

This part of the journey has a new central character, a Weston Rhyn man of influence and distinction.

In his final years he did something his sisters thought was stupid, but it would change The Quinta forever.

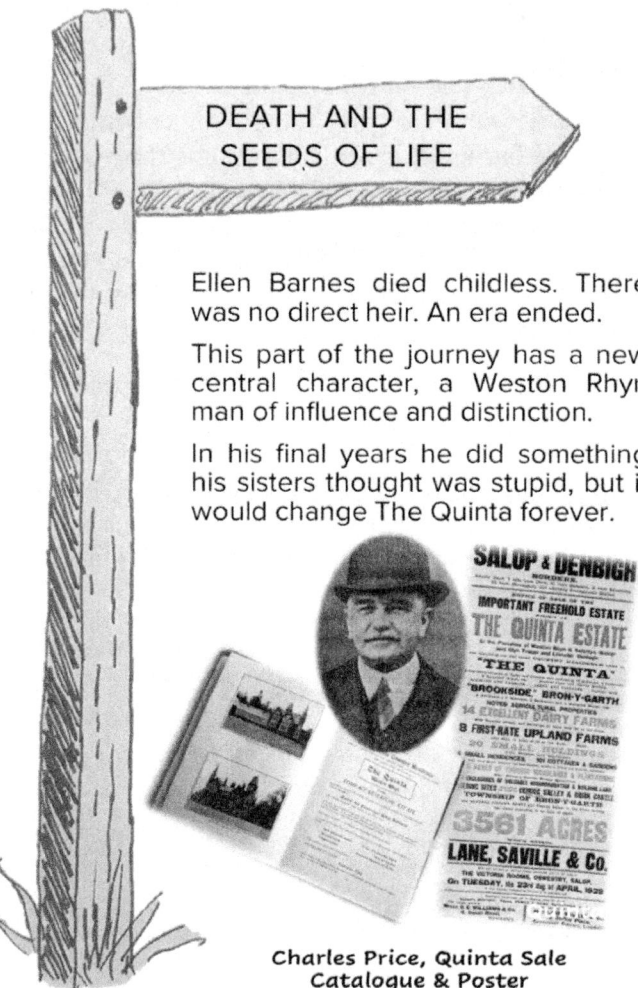

Charles Price, Quinta Sale Catalogue & Poster

QUINTA TIMELINE 1920 1940

Chapter 5
Death and the Seeds of Life

Ellen Barnes' Will

Ellen Barnes wrote her will in 1913, seven years before her death. She appointed people she trusted as her executors. They were deeply familiar with her work. She left almost the entire Quinta estate to the Barnes family, specifically to James' cousin, Harold Barnes. However, Ellen came from a wealthy family and had her own money. Apart from a few specific bequests, she left the majority of her estate in Trust to benefit her many local interests.

When the Ellen Barnes Charitable Trust finally became active in the early 1920s, the Chair of the Trustees was Harold Barnes, to whom she had left The Quinta and who still ran the family cotton business. The other Trustees were another family member, her solicitor, a friend and William Frith, the Quinta Estate Agent. She left the Quinta Church, the Manse, the Bronygarth School and three cottages in the Trust's ownership.

Several other elements of the Barnes family legacy had already been set up as independent charities: The Quinta Sunday Schools, The British Workman's Institute and a Burial Ground. The Trustees were required to invest the bequest and use the annual income for the benefit of such charitable institutions of an educational, religious, or philanthropic nature in the neighbourhood of The Quinta, the Parish of Weston Rhyn or any adjacent Parish as they thought fit. At the Trustees' discretion, Ellen wished to support, in order:

The Bronygarth School
The Quinta Evangelical Free Church
The Quinta Sunday School
The British Workman's Institute (Sometimes known as "The Britannia", its name in its former life as a public house)
Paying the wages of a District Nurse
Any public or private scheme for the benefit of Weston Rhyn and Farnworth

This provision closely followed her lifelong interests and commitments. Despite the passing of 100 years, some of her legacy still survives. The Bronygarth School was handed to the Local Education Authority and later closed. The British Workman's Institute closed after the Second World War. The Quinta Church separated from the Ellen Barnes Trust in 1996 and remains open with very low numbers.

Over the years, the Trust has supported and enabled other local organisations. The Village Institute and the Weston Rhyn Trust, which owns and manages the Village Recreation Ground, are amongst several organisations that owe much to the Ellen Barnes Trust. The Trust also supported schools, hospitals and a wide range of other organisations over the past century. In 1956, the Trust opened six homes for those in need at Quinta Meadows, adjacent to the main entrance of The Quinta. These almshouses remain in use.

Harold Barnes and his family were not interested in keeping The Quinta Estate. In common with thousands of other country estates, its time was over. The houses themselves were too big to maintain. The aristocracy's domination with their large mansions and many servants had ended. The First World War confirmed social changes that were already underway. At the end of the 1920s, the entire estate was put up for sale.

The Sale

Even when many country estates were breaking up, this was a remarkable auction sale. A total of 3,561 acres were to be auctioned. They included no less than 42 farms and smallholdings. There were four small residences, 101 cottages and their gardens, 575 acres of thriving woodland and plantations and 33 enclosures of valuable accommodation and building land. The catalogue was 134 pages long and included photographs and maps. It has become a historical document. Some local families still have copies. The catalogue listed 215 lots, and three pages listed the rents payable on all the properties. The large sale poster is displayed in the Oswestry Town Museum.

It took several sales to clear everything. A note in the family copy of the 1929 Auction Sale catalogue that I borrowed stated, "Quinta Hall and its immediate grounds, Lot 1, will (subject to remaining unsold at the time of the auction) be offered at the upset price of £5,000."

A Timely Intervention

The central character in this part of The Quinta story is Charles Price. He was born in Weston Rhyn in 1857, just after Thomas Barnes had built and moved into Quinta Hall. He would have known the Barnes family all his life. It is possible that Charles was taught in Sunday School by Thomas Barnes himself. Charles worked with Ellen Barnes to raise funds to purchase land and construct the Weston Rhyn Institute. They were both early Trustees. Charles was well known to the Barnes family and shared their values.

Charles was a member of a large family. His father was the village schoolmaster. While most of the family stayed in the village, Charles and two of his brothers had distinguished careers. One was a Harley Street Surgeon. Another brother, Lloyd Turton Price (1873-1933), was a distinguished Scottish surgeon who, among many other roles, was Professor of Surgery at the University of St Andrews.

Charles began working as a salesman for Cadbury. In 1875, he partnered with Robert McVitie, an established Edinburgh biscuit manufacturer. They formed the well-known company McVitie and Price. In 1892, they introduced the famous digestive biscuits. In 1901, Charles retired from active involvement in the company, continuing in a consultative role only. In 1906, he was elected as the Liberal MP for Edinburgh Central. He stayed as an MP until 1918.

Charles was a well-known Parliamentarian and staunch radical. In an obituary by Sir James Leishman, he is described as "Having a keen quality of brain, fast energy and absolute integrity. As a Liberal in good and bad times, he spent his time and money without stint to help his party and his cause as MP for Central Edinburgh. He was frequently referred to as the MP for Edinburgh and even as "The Member for Scotland". Once he took up a subject, he never let go, and departments and ministers regarded him as a perfect terror and burden so much did he goad them into activity."[23] He campaigned especially for war pensions and welfare. He was awarded the distinction of becoming a freeman of the City of Edinburgh. He was also admitted as a Fellow of the Royal Society.

The minister of the Congregational Church in Edinburgh, where Charles was a Deacon for 40 years, described him as "...a choice soul, one of God's good men, a gracious soul, he radiated sunshine and good cheer wherever he went.

That kind of influence was never forgotten."[24]

Charles declined a seat in the House of Lords and returned to Weston Rhyn. There, he continued his work for his local community as his health began to fail in his seventies. When The Quinta Estate came up for sale, he bought Quinta Hall and the residual 52 acres.

Several decades ago, I had a surprise visit from Miss Edwards of Weston Rhyn when I was in the office at Quinta Hall. She explained that she used to be "in service" as a housemaid at the family home, Westlands. Charles returned to Weston Rhyn after retiring from his time in Scotland. She gave me pictures of the Price family and told me about them. It was her clear recollection that Charles' sisters thought he was exceedingly stupid to buy Quinta Hall. What possible use could a small country house have in the early 1930s, when large country houses past their prime were abundant?

Not long after his purchase, Charles died in 1934. He had been in ill health for some years. He left the hall, park and cottages known as The Quinta to be held in trust for "...any religious purpose or purpose connected with the Evangelical Protestant Christian Religion." If no use was found, it was to be sold, and the residue was divided equally between the London Missionary Society and the China Inland Mission.

Charles' motives can only be guessed. Perhaps Charles treasured his memories of the Barnes family. Maybe he could not accept that the 75-year-old building, which had been a home and was also open to Christian and community use, could end up desolate and purposeless. It is safe to say that he would have been astounded to know that before the end of the century, the small country house he left in Trust would become a Christian Conference Centre with over 250 beds and host an international mission, training and relief organisation working all over the world.

FRUIT IN THE WILDERNESS

The Quinta has reached its lowest point. The estate on which so much care was lavished has been sold off.

A little unfairly, I have called the next part of the journey "Fruit in the Wilderness", triggered because it lasts exactly 40 years and contains difficult stories.

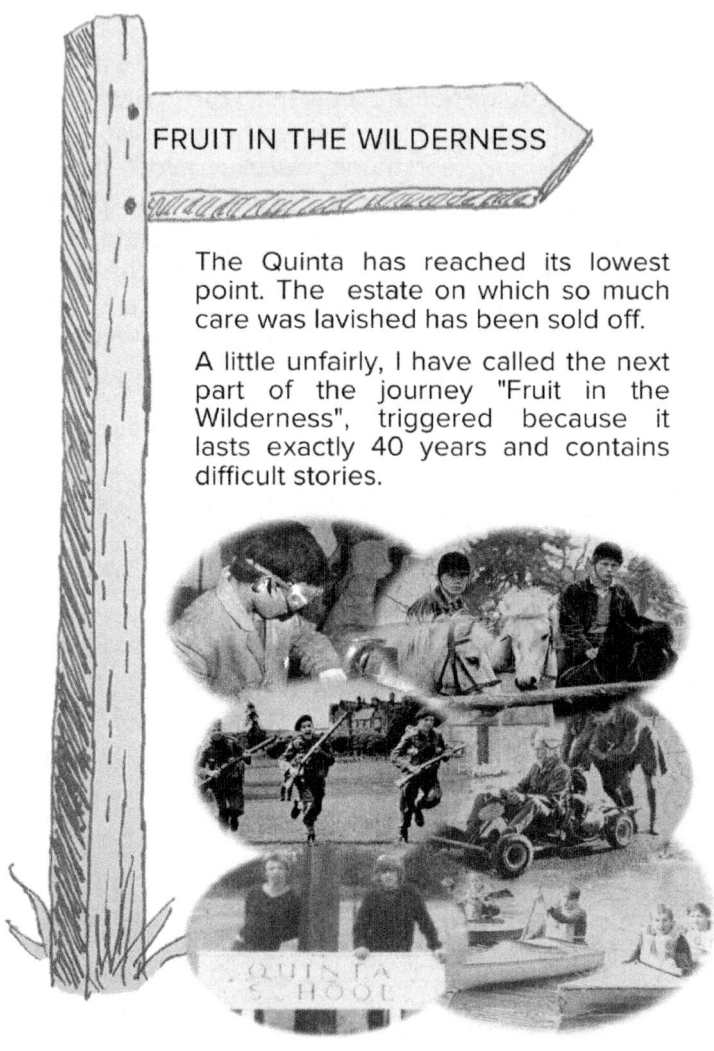

QUINTA TIMELINE 1940 1980

Chapter 6
Fruit in the Wilderness

Wilderness years often pose questions for which ready answers do not exist. Sometimes, they also contain significant changes that lay the foundations for a future you may not have expected. It would be easy to skip this part of the journey, but I invite you to explore the issues revealed.

Many may not be familiar with the history or issues surrounding the care of children and young people in trouble. I will start by providing background information to introduce the lives of those involved in this part of The Quinta's history.

The New Approved School Movement

In the previous century, Reform Schools were started in response to the growing problem of juvenile delinquency in industrial cities. With poor living conditions, many children were drawn into petty crime. So, in 1884, Reform Schools were established as an alternative to prison for children under the age of 16. They reflected the Victorian ideals of moral reform. They were supposed to rehabilitate children through education, discipline and moral guidance. They were often strict, focusing on hard work, religious instruction and vocational training. In 1933, a Children and Young Persons Act replaced Reform

Schools with Approved Schools. This was intended to shift the system towards a more welfare-orientated approach, focusing on education and care. Approved Schools were run by local authorities, charities, or religious organisations and overseen by the Home Office.

In the late 1930s, Barnardo's were either asked or felt it right to volunteer to be involved in the new Approved School movement. They had seen an advert looking for people to use The Quinta and must have felt it would be suitable for progressive work with children who had broken the law. At that time, Barnardo's was an explicitly Christian organisation, so they met the conditions required to become the first Trustees of the Price Trust.

Quinta Hall was architecturally butchered to create the school. What would have been a Grade II* listed building with its Victorian architecture and elaborate internal decoration was ripped apart. The shaped tiled roofs of the water tower and the turret were removed. The Victorian Conservatory and the Billiard Room were demolished, and a crude brick and concrete structure was tacked onto the side. The estate buildings were modified to serve as workshops and very basic schoolroom facilities. Britain was at war then, so setting up a well-equipped Approved School in 1940 would be a country mile from the nation's financial priorities.

In 1941, the Quinta School finally opened as an Approved School, taking 64 boys aged 13-15. There is good reason to believe Barnardo's were at the forefront of trying to advance work with young offenders. The Staff were people of integrity doing their best in a system that was a product of its time: a system that would eventually be found inadequate. In their early days, Approved Schools were regarded as very successful. A personal testimony from a former pupil who visited The Quinta much later in life supports this. He reflected that it was at The Quinta that, for the first time ever, he had a bed to himself and shoes for his feet. Some children came to the Quinta from situations of severe deprivation. Undoubtedly, many good relationships were formed between the Staff and the boys.

An article about the school in the Border Counties Advertizer from 1956 describes the headmaster, Iowerth Isaac, as "...a giant of a man, very tall and massively built with a powerful personality. His fair hair and complexion still gave him a youthful appearance, so he looked like the international rugby player he had been."[25] He had represented the Welsh national teams in rugby union and rugby league. He described to the reporter the value of the boys coming away from dismal, deprived inner-city areas to the country and the healing aspects of rural life. He had tried to replace the previous regime's dull, dark decor with light-coloured schemes. Through this period, the school had a remarkable choir that performed across the area, including at the Llangollen International Eisteddfod. They won many trophies. Graham Wright, MBE, who taught at the school for almost all the forty years it was open, led the choir. His music lessons were "energetic", but the boys held him in high regard. I was very impressed when I heard the choir years later.

Significant Changes

By the 1960s, the weaknesses of the Approved School model were becoming apparent. At some stage, a further extension to Quinta Hall had been made, and the bungalows were built at the bottom of the drive. However, the government made significant funds available to develop the Approved School Model.

In the mid-1960s, two new house units were constructed, each accommodating 30 boys and with staff houses on either end. Homes were built for the senior staff team. There were new classrooms, workshops and a typical 1960s multi-use gymnasium with a stage. There was a certain amount of refurbishment of existing buildings, accompanied by the installation of three new large oil boiler rooms and oil tanks in each main area of the site: Quinta Hall, the new house units and all the various buildings at the top end of the site. It was a massive redevelopment about 100 years after Thomas Barnes built Quinta Hall. Dave, the junior of two local draughtsmen, assisted in drawing all the plans for the new buildings. Their work had to follow detailed specifications provided by the Home Office, which covered the entire development. Dave recollects that the value of the contract was between £300,000 and £400,000.

Considering inflation, the investment would be about six million pounds today.

Legal and administrative changes backed these physical changes. In 1969, another Children and Young Persons Act significantly altered the system. Approved schools became Community Homes with Education. From January 1970, children received Care Orders rather than Approved School Orders.

Critically, the oversight of Community Homes with Education was transferred from the Home Office to the Department of Health and Social Security. They moved from the government department responsible for prisons to the one responsible for social work. Typically, these schools were now run directly by charities, such as Barnardo's, or by local authorities.

These changes reinforced the priority of rehabilitation, education and care over punishment. They took in children who could not live with their families. These children were often also failing at school. At the same time, they continued to take young offenders who received Care Orders as an alternative to custodial sentences. The Quinta School was one of the first to receive this large capital injection for redevelopment. Under Barnardo's guidance, it was amongst those leading the field. A new headmaster, Jim Wilkinson, was appointed. He effectively oversaw the transition from Approved School to Community Home (Education) in the last few years of the 1960s and the early 1970s. The most significant change was in the number and quality of Staff.

In the house units, there would now be four or five residential social work Staff alongside a team of domestic Staff, including cooks, cleaners and Staff responsible for laundry and clothing.

In 1972, in addition to these changes, the school-leaving age was raised from 15 to 16. So, overnight, a parallel switch occurred on the education side. Most Quinta boys were previously in a work-training environment, such as carpentry, metalwork, building, or grounds maintenance. After 1972, they were almost all in school.

The Journey Becomes Personal

I first came to The Quinta in 1971 on a temporary appointment as a housemaster as the changes have described began to consolidate. Let me try to describe it to you.

Starting naive and fresh out of college in this environment, just before the better staffing ratios became a reality, I often found myself on duty alone, responsible for 40 boys. They were all, at this point, subject to Approved School Orders. I had to take them through all life's processes: getting them up, overseeing meals, parading them for school, running activities, supervising free time and putting them to bed. It was challenging. I remember mealtimes. Meals are one of the key events in human life. The dining room, now the main lounge in Quinta Hall, was particularly difficult for a raw recruit. It has four doors, one in each corner of the room, which created great potential for any boy wanting to make mischief at mealtimes. I had to learn how to keep life flowing smoothly.

I soon learned how the system worked. My colleague, who led the House Unit, also ran the most attractive activity in the school: horse riding. Any boy who wanted to be chosen for this prestigious activity would naturally ensure he kept in my colleague's best books. I had nothing to offer at that stage, so I had to learn the hard way.

Life was an incredible mix, from being happily engaged in attractive activities to dealing with the harsh realities of teenagers whose lives had been damaged. There were about 100 boys in the three house units. In the evenings and at weekends, Staff would come on duty and provide activities and interesting things to do. The exception was the Saturday morning two-hour cleaning routine, which involved work for all, including polishing floors, cleaning showers and toilets and sweeping driveways. Yes, the whole drive from top to bottom! It was a real hangover from the Reform School era.

I mentioned the ponies. Julia, the wife of one of the residential Staff, became involved with the ponies. She recollects that it started with the Headmaster's daughter having a pony. The boys took an interest in her and her pony. It was realised that ponies would provide a great activity. So, the school ended up with half a dozen or more.

One boy would be responsible for their overall care: feeding them in the morning, taking them out and putting them back in the evening. Many others enjoyed riding and looking after them in the evenings or on weekends.

Other activities included fishing in the lake or even canoeing on it. Some would play football on the yard or even tennis. The metalwork instructor helped build go-karts which were used on the games field. The school minibuses were used to take boys out all over the place for walks and trips of all kinds. Eric trained in mountain leadership and took boys hill walking in Snowdonia.

In the 1970s, the outdoor activity industry began to take off. Qualifications became important. In contrast, I recall an older, long-serving Staff member saying, "I don't know what all the fuss is about. In the old days, we used to take the whole school of 60 or so boys up Snowden with one Staff member at the front and one at the back." Imagine that today! There was even a small Army Cadet Force consisting of about half a dozen boys. We had a couple of sailing boats. We used Shropshire Education Authority's sailing facilities at Colmere. I did a cave leadership course and, for many years, took boys on simple expeditions to old local slate mines and caves, including the Ogof, the old Roman copper mine at Llanymynech. We took boys out digging for old bottles several times: I still have a bottle collection.

So, there was a very positive, fun side. Julia remembers her husband, Paul, saying, "I can't believe I'm paid to do this." People in the area were quite envious of the activities we provided. Some have recollections of coming up to swim in the very cold outdoor swimming pool. Others played football against the Quinta boys. At one stage, there was even a disco where some local young people came. However, this did not last long.

I need to ground this fun picture in a harsher reality. A few of the boys who had slipped into the system really should not have been in residential care. For example, a boy had been brought up by his grandmother in the Caribbean; at around 11 years old, he was sent to England to join his parents, who had arrived in the Midlands years before. The trauma of this experience triggered problems, and he received a Care Order. He was a lovely boy and became a deeply respected character by all. Fortunately, his Quinta experience stabilised his situation. With a few other boys, he went to the local secondary school. Eventually, he joined the family of a Staff member. It was a great success story.

Most boys faced family and school problems that led to the Care Order process and their removal from home. In many ways, their behaviour was the rational response to their situation. They were not deeply disturbed. They would view the Care Order as a form of punishment. Although damaged by their circumstances, not many were suffering from deeper psychological issues.

They did not want to be away from their home environment, so they resented the system. They would often try to run away.

There were a few boys with more profound psychological problems. A visiting psychiatrist saw a handful of boys regularly. A few of them were put on medication. In those days, the other boys would be wary of their unpredictable behaviour. I recall once being in my classroom on the first floor when one of these boys completely lost it with another boy in my class. He had got a knife, climbed the drainpipe and, hanging on with one arm, was brandishing the knife in the other and screaming at the lad in my class. The Deputy Head was looking on from below and eventually talked him down.

Through the 1970s, the school wrestled with these tensions. I remember the Headmaster being seconded to one of the two senior residential social work courses for one year. While he was away, the Deputy, who had been with the school since it started, was what one might call "old school". In the early days, boys were terrified of him. He could walk into a room, and it would go silent. While the head was away, he reinstated the use of the cane, which had been banned. He did not use it much. However, Eric remembers being called into the study to witness a caning. It stays with him 50 years later: the witnessing of a boy straddled across the desk and receiving six strokes of the cane. Eric was deeply sickened by this experience, let alone the boy.

In the mid-1970s, the school addressed the problem of absconding by using group punishment. If one or two boys ran away, the whole house group would lose their next weekend at home. Worse than this, those boys, on return, had to wear 'shorts and pumps' throughout the day for a few days. Very few absconded. The school was using group pressure to control behaviour. Inevitably, the policy set up the older and bigger boys as enforcers. I remember arguing against this system in a Staff meeting, but the problem was that the system worked. Fortunately, as I recollect, that system was stopped and replaced by a sophisticated system of awarding points across the week so that weekends at home were only lost in a run of continuously extreme individual behaviour.

Comment

Reporting these things is not easy. It is like looking back at an utterly different age. By the time my career in working with troubled children and young people ended in 1985, I had been trained in the behavioural sciences, special education and residential social work. Despite this, I knew virtually nothing of what is known today, some 40 years later. Now, almost every conceivable type of behaviour is categorised. Some are seen as medical conditions, and many recognised educational disorders exist.

The knowledge base for working with people is much more developed and sophisticated. Over the relatively short period of 40 years, a completely new manual for treating children and individuals with problems has been written. So, for many of you looking into this period of The Quinta story, it must be very strange. However, it is worth lingering in our journey through time, as every piece of the story provokes reflections on numerous issues. What has changed? What is better? What is worse? How do we engage with these challenging issues today, especially at a time when the incidence of mental health problems has grown exponentially?

In Summary

To summarise, I pass on the stories of two men who were pupils at The Quinta School. The first, Billy, has written a book titled 'A Reason for Living: The Story that Shocked the World.'[26] Billy had the most horrendous childhood you could possibly imagine. His mother punished him cruelly to the extent that it was not far off the isolated cases of child deaths we still hear of today. On one occasion, at the age of nine, he was locked in a shed with six cats, being fed once a day with bread and water. After nearly a week, the cats started attacking each other and him. He ended up killing the cats. His mother eventually let him out. His story reveals how he concealed his injuries and the harsh reality of his life from his teachers. He got sucked into petty crime to feed himself.

By the time he arrived at The Quinta, he had suffered an extremely damaging upbringing. Looking back, it is patently ridiculous that Staff like me had very little idea of his back story. He did a piece of creative writing in class that, for some reason, I kept with some other work in a box that, in retrospect, should have alerted me to his reality.

In his book, he identified the realities of the control system in the school that I have already described. Somehow, he survived, and I like to think he found some stability. However, when he went home, he had to face the same abuse. His story goes on to describe a half-life of survival. On several occasions, he tried to commit suicide. His reason for living was the birth of a son arising from a relationship with a woman whom he describes as deeply inadequate as a mother. Somehow, after separating, Billy managed to bring up his son. Billy came to my attention many years after the school closed when I received an angry email challenging the notion that a once horrible school could become a Christian Centre. We corresponded. Billy still lives in Birmingham, and we are in marginal contact through Facebook. His story illustrated some of the realities and tensions of the Barnardo's era.

About 15 years ago, another pupil, Brett, rang my doorbell at The Quinta on a Saturday afternoon. He had volunteered to help with his church youth group for their weekend away. Only at the very last minute, too late to pull out, did Brett ask where they were going.

Can you imagine what went through his mind when he learned that it was The Quinta, where he had been sent away for four years by a juvenile court?

His story was something I'll never forget. I recently visited him to review the details. He had shared with Billy a history of abuse at home. At school, he was also frequently beaten. They utterly failed to pick up his learning problems. He remembered being driven to The Quinta for over three hours in his social worker's blue Citroen 2CV. He said he cried for three days.

Interestingly, he did not share my distress about the control the bigger boys exerted over the workings of the school world. It worked for him. Because he was so young, small and vulnerable, one of the senior boys was told by a member of Staff to look out for him. That person, Tony, did just what was asked of him. The system protected Brett. He had been so damaged and traumatised by his school experience that his adverse reaction in the schoolroom was hard to break down. However, it was Brett who was first to recollect the name of his class teacher: Viv. He described Viv as the "best teacher ever" and remembers her with considerable affection.

He also remembers a wonderful world of Quinta activities. He has fond memories of The Quinta. When he visited, he took his son fishing in the lake. With such a challenging home and school background, Brett believes, in hindsight, that leaving home was the best thing for him. He was one of the boys who got to work on the horses.

Eventually, Brett did work experience at a small racing stable not far away from The Quinta. He left and went to Newmarket, where he completed his jockey apprenticeship before going to Marlborough. While a jockey, Brett took up boxing and became the Stable Lads' National Boxing Champion. Eventually, he became a kitchen porter at Marlborough College.

In 1983, he sold up what meagre possessions he had and arranged to go to India on a trip that was to be funded by carrying drugs. With his journey barely started, he was in Clifton, Bristol. There, he had the most extraordinary experience. For about three hours, he had a bizarre set of mental, physical and spiritual experiences defying description in normal language. Voices, pictures in his mind, whatever labels you like to ascribe, forcing him to confront the worst things he had done in his life, sometimes pushing him towards extreme self-harm, but eventually requiring him to make a choice to change his life.

He remembers running and throwing his jacket, which contained his wallet with all his money, into the Clifton Gorge. He spent the night with a student group, just sitting in a basement flat. In the morning, he responded to church bells and went to church. Later, he returned and told the minister he wanted to be a missionary!

The Christian community resettled him in his hometown of Birmingham, where he eventually trained as a carpenter and later established his own business.

Several decades later, he has a great family. He runs a successful business with sixty employees, making high-security doors for government and other buildings. Still active in the church, he is a leading member of Africa-Equip, a charity dedicated to "...giving people in Africa a hand up, not a handout."

Sitting and sharing recollections with Brett in his factory, 50 years after I had been one of his teachers, was an emotional experience for both of us. It exposed both the pains and the joys of these forty years of The Quinta Story.

Another positive was an article I came across in the local paper from 1979 about a string of educational successes by Quinta boys, including CSE passes and credits gained in the City and Guilds Foundation Course in Engineering that we were running.[27] So, with some significant reservations, I look back positively on that era of The Quinta, which I have, in many respects, unfairly referred to as the "Wilderness Years". Under challenging circumstances, many good, ordinary individuals gave their best. Years later, a former pupil visited The Quinta Christian Centre. He told Staff, "The day the Quinta School closed, and he drove down the drive for the last time, was the worst day of his life.

A Postscript to this Part of the Journey

It is now known that some horrendous things happened in the residential childcare world. It was only in 1967 that Barnardo's stopped sending children in care to Australia, a practice they openly and deeply regret. But other terrible things occurred. It was not till the late 1980s that the extent of sexual abuse in the childcare system was revealed.

The Quinta School became marginally involved. The abuse was discovered at the West Midlands Regional Assessment Centre, Tennal School in Birmingham, which sent boys to The Quinta and the other six schools in the region. Several Staff members at Tennal were prosecuted. As a result, a now discredited form of police investigation termed "Fishing" or "Trawling" began. "Operation Orchid," as it was called, eventually cost over £1 million. Every former member of Staff and every former resident at all seven Approved Schools and Community Homes in the West Midlands region that could be located were interviewed. Around 2002, I showed the inquiry team, about half a dozen officers, around The Quinta so that they could get a feel for the place they were investigating. Later, I discussed the investigation with the senior investigating officer. He said that The Quinta came out of their enquiry quite well. There were no prosecutions of Staff from the Quinta School.

WAITING FOR THE FUTURE

It has happened again! The Quinta, was shut down for a third time.

This time, everything was dispersed: people, furniture and equipment. But the site had immensely more potential than in 1850 and 1930.

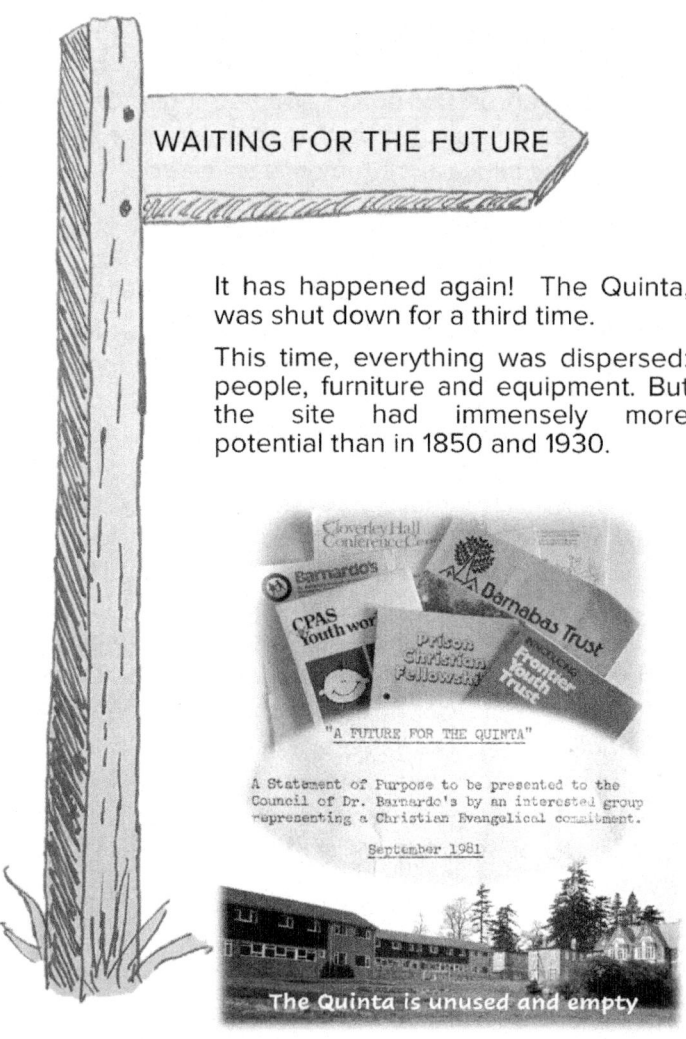

"A FUTURE FOR THE QUINTA"

A Statement of Purpose to be presented to the Council of Dr. Barnardo's by an interested group representing a Christian Evangelical commitment.

September 1981

The Quinta is unused and empty

QUINTA TIMELINE 1980 1985

Chapter 7
Waiting for the Future, Living in the Present

The Closure of the School

The decision to close The Quinta School was made around Easter 1980. Fewer boys were receiving Care Orders that required removal from home, so there were too many of these schools in the region. Quinta was the first to go. Naturally, the Staff were dismayed. We felt, with some justification, that The Quinta School was one of the better schools of its kind and that the decision to close had more to do with politics than the quality of the provision for young people. We made a significant effort to persuade Barnardo's to change The Quinta from a Community Home with Education to a Special School. We researched the possibility, engaged the help of the local MP and wrote to senior Barnardo's executives, but to no avail.

The school was one of the first of its kind to close nationally. There was almost no wisdom and experience to guide the closing process. Barnardo's was very generous to the Staff and promised to maintain salaries until the following March. Everyone imagined it would take a long time to sort things out.

The closure was dramatically faster than expected. There happened to be quite a large cohort of boys who were to reach school-leaving age by the end of the summer term. It was obvious that they should leave then. For the remainder, it became clear that, since their programme was to be disrupted anyway, it was in their interest to move on to their new placement as soon as possible. So, within a few months, we realised that by September, there would only be about a dozen boys left, with a potential staff-to-pupil ratio of four to one. The final closure was rescheduled for the end of 1980.

Sharing an Idea

Please bear with me as I take you deeper into my experience of these years. Besides the fact that individual stories add depth and flavour to the twists and turns of history, I knew firsthand much of what was happening. I can take you through the headlines.

Barnardo's honoured their promises to staff. I was among a few who suggested we could pursue further training rather than simply staying at the school and doing very little. Barnardo's supported us. The calculation was that beyond March, we would have enough money to cover ourselves till the course ended and we got a new job. In the autumn, before the school finally closed, I began commuting to the University of Birmingham to study for a further degree in special education. What a delight to sit in a room after nine years of teaching and let somebody else be responsible for the session. Earlier, just after the final decision to close was made, everyone had a vague idea that The Quinta was held in some Christian Trust. Initially, Barnardo's believed they could sell the school. Fairly early on, a sale had been arranged with a potential buyer.

However, I became burdened that there could be an opportunity for The Quinta to be used for Christian purposes. We were, of course, all mulling over our futures and wondering what would happen. One day, I was gardening and listening to a tape a friend had brought back from Spring Harvest. A British Youth for Christ speaker was launching an initiative, 'A Decade of Evangelism.' He made a remark that struck me: "God was raising up resources for this." This was what prompted me to invite two friends, one, Tony, the rector of St John's Whittington, and the other, Derek, the pastor of The Quinta Church, to write to Christian organisations, stating that we believed there was a possibility that The Quinta could be used for Christian purposes. If we were correct, an extremely useful asset was available.

The immediate outcome was a site meeting in Quinta Hall, attended by approximately a dozen people, including representatives from various organisations and local residents. Scripture Union and British Youth for Christ were involved from the start. As an afterthought, I invited a representative from the nearest Christian Conference Centre, Cloverley Hall. Their Director, John, came to the meeting. He was the ideal person for this situation with his numerous connections, entrepreneurial drive and vision. He became the Chair of the group commissioned in October 1980 to represent a burgeoning interest from what would become a consortium of groups to follow up on the possibility of using The Quinta. This executive group would meet on and off for the next four years as John and one or two others negotiated directly with Barnardo's and the Charity Commission. I took up the role of secretary to the group. We gradually became more confident in the validity of our claim that The Quinta should continue to be used for Christian purposes.

By September 1981, the group had produced an 11-page document for the Council of Barnardo's. It described the group's identity, outlined their vision for using The Quinta, and covered other legal, financial, organisational and practical matters. Five appendices were attached, including a list of supporting organisations and four submissions from key organisations: British Youth for Christ, Frontier Youth Trust, A Christian Concern for the Mentally Handicapped and Prison Christian Fellowship.

The list of supporting organisations was impressive: The Scripture Union, The Church Pastoral Aid Society, City Missions from Birmingham, Manchester and London, The Covenanter Union, The Barnabas Trust, Birmingham Christian Projects, Jesus Centre Birmingham, Christian Mountain Centre, Buzz and Family Magazines, Mission for Christ, Cloverley Hall Conference Centre and the two missions named in the original Price Trust: The Overseas Missionary Fellowship, previously known as the China Inland

Mission, and The Council for World Mission, previously known as the London Missionary Society.

The momentum had been incredible. Many people had become involved and were praying for the initiative. John recollects speaking to Barnardo's Council. He was graciously received as he pointed out that their primary responsibility under the terms of the Price Trust was to ensure The Quinta continued to be used for Christian purposes.

At the end of chapter two, I referred to the future involvement of a Myddelton heir. David Myddelton's father, Ririd Myddelton, sold Chirk Castle to the Welsh Office, who passed it on to the National Trust. David and his wife, Christine, who lived near Chirk Castle, had become Christians. They worshipped at the same church as we did and were also members of our house group. They were very supportive throughout this time. Later, David would offer advice when the new centre opened. As with other details, this was yet another delightful connection across the years in this journey through The Quinta's history.

My Personal Exile

By this time, later in 1981, I had enjoyed my course at Birmingham and had landed what I thought was a great job. Two jobs at Leicestershire's Community Home [Education], Polebrook House, attracted me. They were completely rebuilding the site with six small house units for up to 12 young people each and two specialised units: a secure unit and an intensively staffed linked unit. I joined the senior staff team and was responsible for the two specialised units.

I want to share the details of the day leading up to my interview. I was travelling back to Birmingham in our camper van for a seminar. Halfway down the A5, the main drive shaft broke. As it happened, Derek, who was a signatory to the original letter, passed by, stopped and gave me a lift to Birmingham.

I had missed the seminar, so I decided to catch up on my bible-reading plan. This just happened to be the passage in Jeremiah containing his letter to those held captive in Babylon. He reassured them that their exile was part of God's plan. God knew his plans for them. They were to get on with their lives. He promised that they would enjoy prosperity and eventually return home. Many have read these verses at a significant time in their lives. For me, with an interview the next day, they were a reassuring thought, but in the light of what would happen, they were amazingly prophetic. I could write a fascinating book about what happened over the next four years. Instead, I shall summarise it in a couple of paragraphs, even though I still have two A4 box files struggling to contain all the papers and newspaper cuttings from that time.

Sydney Jones, MBE, was the Principal of Polebrook House. He was a remarkable Christian man who was abandoned as a baby and raised in care.

Some of that experience was bad. Syd was passionately committed to caring for young people and could empathise deeply with them. If we could not do this challenging work under his leadership with these brand-new, specially designed facilities less than 10 miles from the centre of Leicester, then no one could.

I spent my first year overseeing the completion of the new special units and preparing them for opening. The most important part of this was recruiting suitable Staff. We ran one of the most successful recruiting campaigns ever for this specialist work. We asked County Hall to issue employment contracts for approximately 20 new Staff members to start in August 1982. Then we went off to the summer camp.

The annual school camp was great. Syd took the whole school on a week-long holiday and activities trip to the Dyffryn Arddudwy Boys' Brigade site on the Welsh coast near Barmouth. Syd had developed such an ethos for the camp that he only took Staff who volunteered to go, and not all volunteers were taken. Upon our return, we discovered that, during our absence, the Liberal group on the County Council had switched its support from the Conservative Party to the Labour Party. Almost the first decision of the new administration was to stop the opening of the two specialist units at Polebrook. The following week, I had to welcome all the new Staff, some of whom had relocated with their families to the area, with the devastating news that they might not have the job they had come for.

I can only leave to your imagination the things that followed over the next four months as we discovered that the County Council would only make one element of a decision every month. It was four to five months before those new staff members were redeployed across the county to jobs they had not come to Leicestershire for. I made some very good friends in this period of adversity. We soldiered on for another two years before the County Council decided to close the rest of these brand-new units and redeploy us all.

I spent about three months on gardening leave before being redeployed to work with one other person to manage the remaining 22 children's homes across the county. It was chaos. Many of the homes felt they were on the list for closure. Some homes had to cope with very difficult young people on remand with whom they had no experience. It was traumatic for all involved. So much for God's plans for my prosperity!

Although this is out of sequence, I will conclude this brief personal excursion from the main Quinta Story. The pain of this experience stayed below the surface for many years. When I left, I wrote to the Director of Social Services asking for something to be done about the chaos. Several years later, the head of one of the larger homes, who had been feted in the social work press and by local politicians, was prosecuted for the sexual abuse of Staff and children. This led eventually to my being summoned as a witness to the Kirkwood Inquiry.[28] My departing letter had exonerated me while all my colleagues were subsequently held to account by the national press. When you find yourself in a dark place, you must do your best to blow the whistle. Should I have done more?

The Inquiry helped me put that time to bed. But what of God's plans for me? Had these also been chaos and confusion? By the time I returned to The Quinta, I had received years of training in residential work. I had the rare academic distinction of gaining admission to university by mistake: they sent me the wrong letter! I studied what was then known as Personnel Management at Aston University's Department of Industrial Administration. This was complemented by specialist training in education and residential work, topped off by approximately 15 years of practical experience, during which I encountered some of the best and worst practices and practitioners in challenging residential environments. What better preparation could I have for what was about to happen? My boss in Leicestershire used the phrase "thick file person" to describe Staff who were quite capable but needed a lot of care, support and direction to produce good work. Like many others, I am a very "thick file Christian". So, I can testify that God absolutely knew the plans he had for me.

Back to the Main Story

Throughout the period from 1982 to 1984, the group attempting to secure a Christian future for The Quinta continued to negotiate. At one stage,

Barnardo's suggested they could sell half of the estate and give the other half to the consortium of Christian organisations to accommodate their responsibilities as Trustees of the Price Trust. One unresolved issue that hung over negotiations concerned the government funds used to rebuild The Quinta in the 1960s. Whether the government would want their money back and on what terms was unknown. Therefore, anyone who took over from Barnardo's would have to take on the potential liability of repaying this money. This would have been particularly significant if the value of the investment had appreciated in line with the rising value of the property. It could be a very substantial amount of money.

As time passed, most of the negotiations were done by John and Joe. Joe was a Trustee of the Barnabas Trust, a Christian Outdoor Activity provider now known as "Rock UK". The original members of the steering group local to The Quinta were less involved. One of Joe's Barnabas colleagues was John Horne of Horne Brothers, a national men's clothing retailer of the time. I remember meetings in a room above their London store on Oxford Street. On one occasion, John and Joe went to a lot of trouble to produce an attractive brochure with ground plans and drawings to show the Charity Commission how we could use the site. When they arrived at the meeting, they found that the Charity Commissioner involved was blind.

Eventually, early in 1985, John heard from the Charity Commission that we could have The Quinta. A memorable emergency meeting was called in London. The four or five representatives of organisations around the table were all delighted with the outcome. However, as we went around the table, one by one, they stated that their organisation could not be involved at this time. They had committed funds elsewhere or decided it was not right for them.

The only exception was John. He reported they had just finished developing and paying for a new centre, Castlewellan Castle, in Northern Ireland. For the first time ever, they had £40,000 in the bank. He offered to take on The Quinta on behalf of the Christian Community. At the very least, £40,000 would cover the cost of simply holding the estate for a year. If nothing transpired, they would undertake to sell the site and distribute the proceeds as Charles Price had directed in his will.

This was a deeply embarrassing situation. After all the interest generated, the long list of supportive organisations, and four years of work, this site with incredible potential was there for the taking. But we had no plans; we just had one small organisation saying they would give it a go and sell it if nothing happened!

AN OPEN DOOR

The door was open to walk in.

Yet, after four years of schemes and dreams by a consortium of organisations, all the plans had just fallen to pieces.

Within weeks amazing things happened.

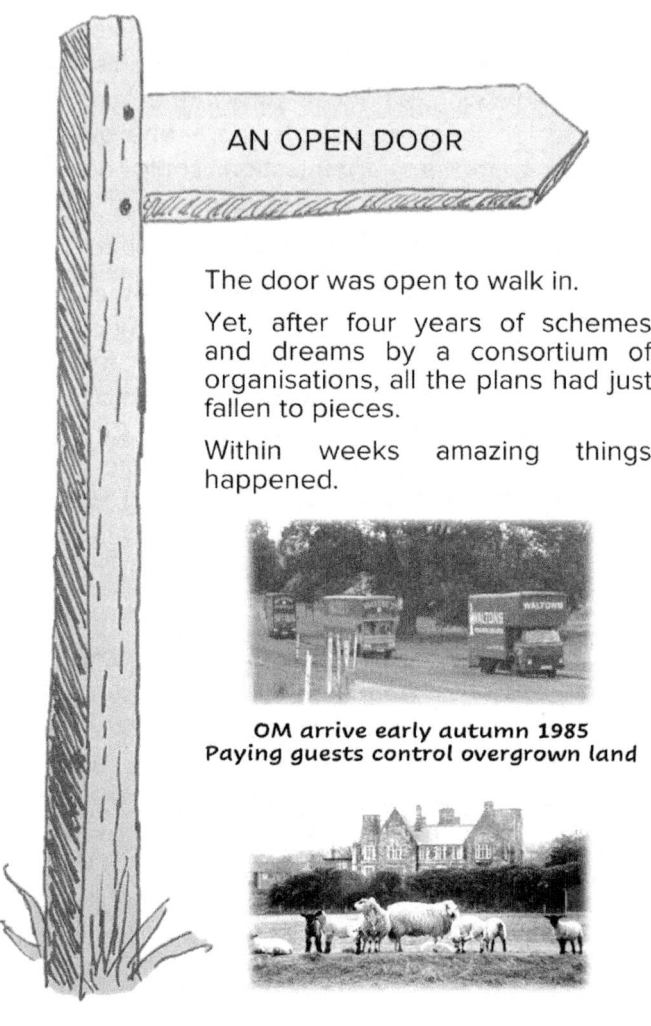

**OM arrive early autumn 1985
Paying guests control overgrown land**

QUINTA TIMELINE 1985 .... c. 1990

Chapter 8
An Open Door

At this stage, The Quinta story verges on the realm of fiction. Early in 1985, an extensive former Victorian country house with 52 acres of land, two purpose-built residential units, a theatre/gymnasium, a range of classrooms and workshops, numerous outbuildings and over a dozen housing units sat completely empty, awaiting use. However, after four years of schemes and dreams by a consortium of responsible organisations, all the plans had fallen to pieces. Cloverley Hall, later renamed "Centre Ministries", agreed to take it on and see what happened.

The formalities would take almost a year to complete. It was not until 9 December 1985, that Centre Ministries, itself a registered charity, became the Corporate Trustees of the Price Trust and, therefore, still now owns the Quinta under the terms of the Trust. However, Barnardo's allowed the new Christian Centre to start before the legal transfer was completed.

A significant development occurred within weeks of the announcement that we could proceed. It is one of the most extraordinary stories we will encounter on our journey, so it is worth examining the details. Tony was the Director of Operation Mobilisation UK.

Their central office for their worldwide mission, training and relief work was close to Manchester city centre. Tony's notes from the time tell the story:

"In the 1970s and 1980s, the UK Headquarters of Operation Mobilisation was located at 142 Dantzic Street, Manchester, in an old Victorian building known as the Charter Street Mission. We were indebted to the Trustees of the Mission for letting us use their premises rent-free.

Not only were the offices situated here, but there was also accommodation for all the single team members and one married couple. The offices, mailroom, team meeting room and lounge, kitchen, team dining room and a linked Christian printing press were contained within the building with room to spare. Many vast spaces were unoccupied, and one had been turned into a Badminton Court. The place was old, tired and dirty, yet the team held it in affection. A visitor in 1985 described it:

"The building was massive, and with its red brick construction, it looked awful. It was bounded by roads on three sides and a high-level railway on the fourth, with the huge St Michael's burial ground adjacent. The words "Working Girls Home" were carved into the stone above the entrance. The same legend greeted you in a floor mosaic as you entered, with the door on the left bearing the word "MATRON". The windows were rotting and in danger of falling out, and the whole place needed attention. To reach the offices, one had to climb to the top (third and fourth) floors, part of which used to be a vast dormitory space with a high ceiling. It was so cold and barn-like that they had created makeshift offices, resembling "shacks", in this huge room. Because the roof leaked all over, buckets were positioned on the roofs of these offices to catch the water.

In other parts of this vast building were bedrooms for the single men and women on the team, with a bathroom for each section. The two massive, cast-iron, enamelled baths in the girls' section looked as if they had been there since the place was built. The sides were so high that you almost needed steps to get into them. On the floor beneath the office space was another equally large space that the team had converted into a badminton court, which they used every lunchtime. Below that, on the ground floor, was a church meeting hall."

I can vouch for this because I visited Dantzic Street before OM left. It was just as the visitor said. Because it was a former residential home, I was familiar with this type of building. I instantly recognised the top floor in its previous life as a vast dormitory. I will never forget the crude shacks they had built inside this huge top-floor room, with buckets on top to catch the rainwater dripping from the roof.

Tony's story continues: "In the June 1983 General Election, one of the British team members registered to vote, using the Dantzic Street address as her home address." Her registration went through okay, but the application brought us to the attention of the local authorities. They did not have our address as a place of residence. As a result, over the next two and a half years, we were visited by representatives from various local authority departments, including the rates office, the fire safety office and others. Over the course of two years, they updated their information. This included spending months updating their building plans, which encompassed stairwells, means of escape and numerous other aspects. They eventually presented us with a rates bill and a schedule of work that we had to complete within six months to ensure that the building met all the up-to-date fire and safety standards. Failing to complete the schedule meant that we had to vacate the premises.

We commissioned an architectural survey of the property. After obtaining quotes for the work involved to meet the local authority requirements, plus the minimum refurbishment work needed to bring the premises up to a basic standard, i.e. stop the roof leaks, replace rotten windows, etc., it was evident that not only did we not have the money needed, but the value of the building (which of course we didn't own) at that time was less than the estimated costs of the work. Also, because of its location, being trapped between roads and railway viaducts, and its size compared to the small footprint of the building, the cost of demolition was higher than the value of the land it sat on.

In February 1985, at a Board Meeting on board MV Doulos in Sunderland, we decided not to invest in the Dantzic Street property.

This decision inevitably meant that we would have to vacate the building. Although I had been granted a six-month extension to keep the offices open for a little longer, I had to close the accommodation within a few days.

I explained to the team what had happened and asked them to pray for God's provision while they travelled back to Manchester in the minibus. We had no idea where to look for rent-free accommodation. I later learned that, while praying, the team decided to make a list of requirements. As they put this list together, it grew from requirements to aspirations and from aspirations to dreams. They didn't tell me until later that it included a house in the country, a gymnasium, tennis courts, a swimming pool, somewhere to keep a horse, etc.

A couple of days later, I was returning from Doulos by train only to have it break down in Woodhead Tunnel, where I sat in darkness for two hours with nothing to do but cry out to God for His intervention. When I finally got home, there were two phone calls that I needed to reply to that evening. The first was from Doug Saddler, who represented the Overseas Missionary Fellowship in the Northwest but knew nothing about our accommodation crisis. He thanked me for calling back and asked if I could use a large old manse that had been available for six months, which he had just heard about. I couldn't believe it. It was big enough to meet all our immediate accommodation needs and was within easy travelling distance to the office!

We started moving the team out. Within the local authority deadline, we had completely vacated the residential part of Dantzic Street.

The second phone call was from a gentleman who attended West Street Baptist Church in Crewe. I met him at a church outreach weekend we had taken about a year before. He had phoned up on a personal matter, but towards the end of the conversation, he asked me if I had ever inquired about an empty country house that he had mentioned to me all those months before. I didn't remember the conversation, probably because it was irrelevant to me at the time. Now, my ears picked up, and he said he would get me a contact to call by the next day.

Sure enough, the following morning, he left a phone number and the name Rev. John Rosser, a person I had never heard of. I picked up the phone with fear and trepidation and told John of our predicament, explaining who I was. After a stunned silence, he explained that for the last five years, he had headed a coalition of Christian organisations attempting to take over the Price Trust, which had responsibility for The Quinta estate, from Barnardo's. Each organisation had dropped out one by one, leaving only the conference ministry based at Cloverley Hall, which John headed up. John was about to travel to London for a meeting where the coalition would be formally dissolved, leaving Centre Ministries to take a step of faith in assuming control of the Price Trust.

He explained how he had always had a fond link with OM and asked how quickly I could see The Quinta.

The next day, Rex Worth and I travelled to Shropshire to be met by Rev. Derek Baines, the minister of the Quinta Church. He fed us and then took us to look around The Quinta. We were lost for words! It had everything that we needed and more. When we returned to tell the team what we had seen, they couldn't believe that every item on their "prayer list" was there. In fact, when we moved, one of the girls even brought her horse with her. John Rosser then invited us to tell him which properties we would like to use."

OM was to occupy almost all the properties built in the 1960s south of Quinta Hall. They had the two house-unit blocks: one would be their office block and the other an accommodation block. In addition to the four semi-detached houses on either end of these blocks, they had four more houses, some garages and a few outbuildings.

While this was happening, I was still navigating the chaos of Leicestershire's residential care for children and young people. I was excited by the development at The Quinta. I wanted to return and help the new Centre come to life. Jenni was reluctant to return to a place we had left five years earlier. However, we agreed I would volunteer for a two-year appointment as a Project Manager to get the new Centre up and running. I resigned, and our house sold so fast that we were almost made homeless waiting for the final permission to move on-site.

On Thursday, 4 July 1985, we arrived and camped overnight in the house on the drive allocated to us. Our son Tim was 18 months old, and Jenni was four months pregnant. The next morning, the two caretakers who had looked after the site for Barnardo's for the past four and a half years came to the house with an old army-style ammunition box. It was heavy enough for them to need to share the load. It was about three-quarters full of keys: hundreds of them. They said they had switched the water on and were going. Their jobs were redundant. I was now responsible for all the property, including security, the weekly mowing of approximately five acres, and all the other tasks they had previously performed. We were meant to be on holiday for the rest of the month with time to settle into our house!

Our furniture arrived a few hours later. Within a day or so, people from OM arrived to begin work on their buildings. First, to sort out the basic plumbing so that the water and heating systems worked, and then to rewire one block to convert former bedrooms into offices and set up an integrated computer system. We also had the Director of "A Cause for Concern", who, having heard about the other organisations backing out, was considering renewing their interest in using the bungalows at the bottom of the drive as a care home.

We had a hectic holiday, sorting out our home, offering hospitality and maintaining the estate. On July 28th, I sent a newsletter to all our supporters. I wrote:

"Moving, at its best, is hectic, but moving the day after finishing work in Leicestershire onto a large estate that has been unoccupied for four and a half years is even more fun. The list of high-priority jobs is potentially frightening, and many things simply have to be left for the time being. There is a deep sense of peace available because the events of the last four months have assured all concerned of the Lord's control in large and small things alike. Whilst we are clear that now is the time for hard work, we know there is no need to worry about the problems that arise. We have a deep knowledge that the redevelopment of The Quinta, however daunting a task, is one of the millions of links in the wider chain of God's purposes. Despite our inadequacy, it is a real privilege to share with you the joy of being involved. The following pages of news will, we trust, leave you with a sense of excitement and praise."

Bob, reflecting 40 years later from his home in the USA, wrote: "The facilities at The Quinta were beyond our wildest dreams. In the summer of 1985, I led a team of short-term volunteers who cleaned and painted the new OM UK headquarters. I also prepared for the installation of the computer system. I found time to do some cosmetic repairs on the house at 2 Lake View, which would be our family home for the next six years.

My family camped, using our sleeping bags on the floor. In August, our family returned briefly to Manchester to pack our belongings and help load a large, hired lorry with our family's few possessions, as well as some office furniture and equipment. Even though my family had only lived at the Quinta for a few weeks, as I drove that big lorry up the Quinta drive, I felt like we were coming home! I supervised the office computer system during the following years at the Quinta. Many portions of the software had to be adapted. We made many wonderful friends while working at The Quinta and look back on that time as one of the high points of our lives and ministry."

Meanwhile, in August, we had our first group of guests. The Oswestry Community Church came for their annual summer camp. Their pastor was Tony, one of the signatories to the original letter about using The Quinta. When you have 52 acres, managing the land is one of your most urgent priorities. We negotiated two grass keeps with a local farmer and one with a pony-trekking establishment. In the early months, Nick, who stayed with us for two months, helped us erect nearly a mile of fencing and put in two cattle grids.

During the summer, OM completed its initial work with volunteer teams. Again, Tony writes: "...finally, on 18 September 1985, our office moved from Manchester to The Quinta. By early November, we had almost 80 people in residence. Eventually, most of these would move out to join teams all over the world, leaving a small HQ team of around 30 people, including families. A short time later, these numbers increased when the first International Software Development team was formed at The Quinta to create what would become the Petra International Software system for processing donations and the mission's finances.

What started out looking like a major crisis, God had turned into an incredible blessing that enabled our work to grow and change, unfettered by the limits that the Dantzic Street premises would have imposed. God is very good!"

By November 1985, A Cause for Concern had confirmed its intention to convert the four bungalows into long-term homes for those with learning disabilities. Centre Ministries had decided to use Quinta Hall and the former schoolroom and workshop buildings to develop self-catering accommodation, complementing their full-board accommodation at Cloverley Hall.

We had already advertised this even though the buildings were, in effect, derelict. In Quinta Hall, the kitchen walls were black with mould. A parquet floor in what was to be the dining room had been flooded. Part of this floor had risen to make a round mound two feet high and four in diameter. Many rooms still had garish wallpaper and brightly coloured walls from the 1960s to 1970s. There were no carpets, no curtains and no furniture. Most of the bedrooms were large, dormitory-sized rooms.

In the autumn, I showed a group around this derelict facility. They had been involved in Christian holiday conferences at Southwold under the leadership of the evangelist and author Roy Hessian, but this was changing. To my astonishment, they booked Quinta Hall and camping for three weeks the following summer, intending to bring 100 to 200 people each week, with the main meetings being held in a marquee. We had very little money, one staff member [me!] and a nine-month deadline. At a relatively early stage, there was a knock on the door one Sunday afternoon.

Eddie, whom I had never met or heard before, explained that he had heard about The Quinta several times that week and thought he should visit. He had recently managed a large Christian conference centre in North Wales. He and his assistant manager had uncovered that the owner was playing off multiple bank accounts against each other to keep the Centre afloat. They were dismayed by this, and both of them resigned. Eventually, his assistant, Mel, and his family moved to the Quinta. This gave me some high-quality, experienced assistance. But they had already applied to emigrate. Sadly, after a few years, they left for Australia, taking with them fond memories. There is now a house named "Quinta" in Australia.

The winter of 1985-86 was cold and dry. This suited our main job of decorating right through Quinta Hall. David, from Cloverley Hall, brought two or three staff members across two or three days a week throughout most of the winter to help. This was at some significant cost to their work at Cloverley. With David and John's assistance, it fell to me to furnish and equip the Centre. Almost all the furnishings were second-hand ex-hotel stock. I remember David arranging furniture deliveries: one large van with a large trailer attached arrived with about 90 beds and mattresses to be carried to their rooms.

I became familiar with various auctions, especially War Department and Catering Auctions. Some of the ex-military dining room tables are still in use. Happily, over the next 40 years, almost all the remaining second-hand items were to be replaced as funds became available. This included the second-hand carpets. I learned about fitting old carpets and seaming them together. Fortunately, one of the volunteers who came to decorate just happened to be a carpet fitter.

The secret of using a second-hand kit is to do your best to match things.

So, whilst it may look somewhat tired, it does not feel like a junk shop. Looking back. I am amazed at what was done with so little in such a short time. Somehow, we managed to produce a tolerably acceptable venue for our guests. Unlike some new ventures, we did not raise funds. With very little advertising, we received as many bookings as we could handle. This was remarkable.

In the context of Quinta's history, our first booking in Quinta Hall in May 1986 was extraordinary. In fact, it was so improbable that it would not be included in a work of fiction, as it would undermine the story's credibility.

The first group to use the new conference facility was the Chinese Overseas Christian Mission staff conference. You will recall that our benefactor, Charles Price, stipulated that if no use was found for The Quinta, he wanted the property sold and the proceeds given to missions. One of these was the China Inland Mission. The guest speaker of our first group in Quinta Hall just happened to be Dr Leslie Lyall, a former Director of this mission. Imagine telling Charles Price in 1934, long before worldwide air passenger flights existed, that in 52 years, The Quinta would not only have become a centre for worldwide mission but that its first guests would be Chinese people. It is as though someone is having a good laugh! Later that year, they organised a Christmas house party for Chinese students, at which it was claimed that 15 of them became Christians.

Leslie Lyall being the first guest speaker at the new conference facility was to prove even more significant. As you will see later (Chapter 11, 'A Cast of Thousands'), students constitute one of Quinta's most prominent user groups. While he was a student leader at Cambridge in 1928, Leslie Lyall was one of the key people involved in setting up the student Christian movement, then known as the "Inter-Varsity Fellowship".[29]

In those early years, both organisations began consolidating their work at The Quinta. They were joined by a Cause for Concern, which opened its new home in the bungalows at the bottom of the drive after the others had started.

In many ways, it was OM that changed the most. As Tony already mentioned, their new home gave them real potential for their work to grow and mature. Their new offices represented an exponential improvement over the indoor shacks at Dantzig

Street. The digital world was expanding fast. The software developed at The Quinta laid the foundation for the administration of their expanding work worldwide. Interestingly, the Dantzig Street mentality governed their negotiations before they took up residence.

I remember a long-serving OM'er telling me that OM would do anything, provided they didn't have to pay for it. So, a complex agreement was negotiated, and they paid a peppercorn rent for their buildings on a full-repairing lease. They also committed to taking a practical share in looking after and contributing to the cost of the parts of the estate that neither organisation used solely for its own purposes. The understanding was that OM would help with the practical work on the areas held in common.

However, you can imagine the reaction of a computer analyst working hard on new software being asked to go out and dig for a water leak in the rain. It did not take us long to realise that the system would not work, but coming to that conclusion was difficult for both organisations. It also emerged that OM used the common areas less than they initially thought. It does not take much imagination to see the potential for conflict.

The other complication in the early days was that the organisations shared facility meters. Water and electricity bills were calculated using residence statistics. You can imagine the quiet removal of electric fires and energy-greedy kits in both organisations once separate meters were installed:

we are all human! We worked through all these things and emerged with a stronger bond between the two organisations based on deep mutual respect and the desire to enable each other to focus on their own priorities. Additionally, those relatively minor growth pains helped negotiate the new arrangements. OM now only pays rent for a full-repairing lease based on a share of the cost of maintaining the estate, with a formula linked to inflation and the number of people they have. This cost-based arrangement is massively cheaper than commercial rent.

PETER BEVINGTON

RESOURCED TO SERVE

Three organisations have moved in but it takes many years to make The Quinta fit for purpose.

Some things just fell into place, others took many years of hard work.

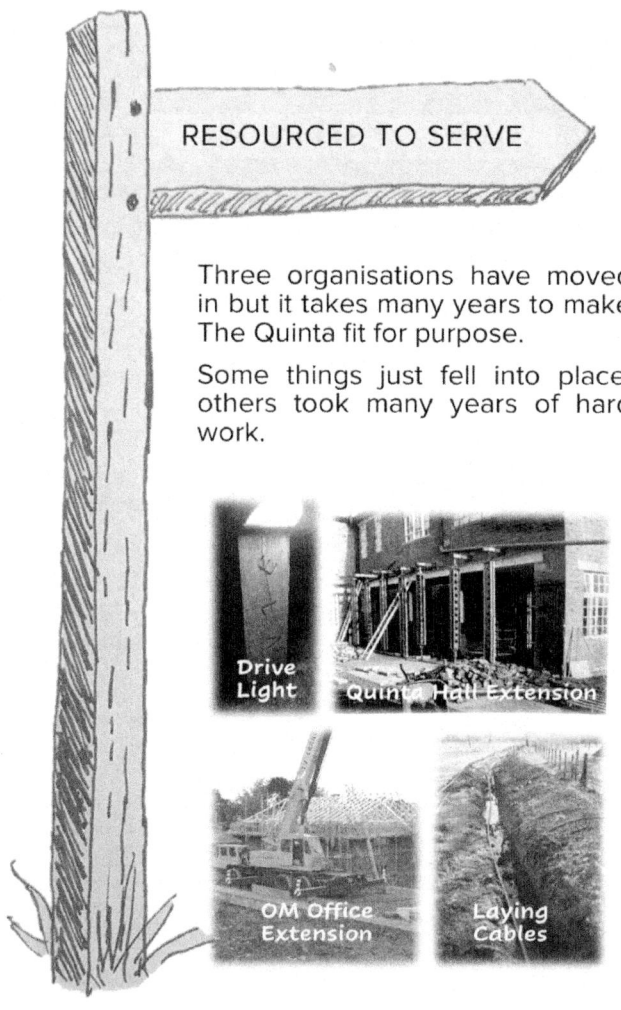

QUINTA TIMELINE c. 1990 .... c. 2005

Chapter 9
Resourced to Serve

There has always been a tendency to split the spiritual from the physical. This false division is still alive and well, but the Quinta reality is that they are intricately integrated. However, in this part of the journey, the focus is on telling the story of the development of the physical resources we tend to take for granted. The way this unsung but absolutely vital infrastructure came together, almost behind our backs, is just another remarkable element in this remarkable story.

Freed from Potential Debt

Some years after moving on-site, we heard extremely important news. Earlier in the journey, I had indicated that anyone taking over The Quinta would have to indemnify Barnardo's against liability for debt repayment to the government if it were decided that the government money used to develop the site in the 1960s had to be repaid. If it had to be repaid, and the repayment also included the property's appreciating value, that would have been a very substantial sum.

A test case was taken to the House of Lords for a ruling. There were many closed Approved School premises across the UK. Some, especially in the Southeast, were considerably more valuable than

The Quinta. The "Finnart House Case" determined that the government investment could not benefit from the appreciating value of these properties.[30] In addition, it was my understanding that organisations like Barnardo's had been routinely paying off the investment loan and that Barnardo's, as it happened, had just finished paying off the loan!

This is perhaps the most sensational aspect of the entire Quinta Story. The buildings that Charles Price left in Trust had been exponentially expanded at government expense. All this was completely free!

Utilities

There is a five-square-metre brick building that most visitors will never notice. I even failed to point it out when I explained all the new buildings created in the 1960s. (Chapter 6, 'Fruit in the Wilderness') Yet this small building, whose door is rarely opened, is an important asset. Not many country houses or small estates, like The Quinta, have their own substation.

As the new Centre geared up for effective ministry, we discovered that almost every area of the estate was underpowered. Gradually, new cables were laid out in all directions. Without a substation on site, this would have been much more expensive and difficult. These mundane things are so important.

We were so blessed with this kind of resource, which made all the difference to what people could do.

We inherited three large boiler rooms with oil boilers, all covered in brown asbestos that had to be removed. There were two large oil tanks with each set of boilers. One set heated the main OM buildings, another heated Quinta Hall and one heated the former workshops, classrooms and sports hall. The memory of ringing around the oil distributors trying to knock 0.1p or so off a litre of heating oil is somewhat amusing now that we are used to paying five or six times more three decades later. The management of utilities and their costs is always a big issue on a large site like The Quinta.

One important development we had no control over was the introduction of mains gas to Weston Rhyn in the early 1990s. Due to the size of The Quinta, the network was extended from the Centre of the village and terminated on the estate. All the boilers were converted to gas, which was cheaper and easier to use and manage.

An immediate and significant side benefit was that we were allowed to put new water pipes in the same trenches. This meant we could lay a completely new water distribution system for the whole estate at the same time. The old system was in various states of disrepair. Leaks were an issue. It also resolved another problem.

As with electricity in the early days, the only way to distribute the cost of water between the three organisations had been to maintain a register of people on site and bill each user accordingly. With the new water distribution system, each building had its own water meter. There was also an unmetered fire hydrant system, which the water company had asked us to turn off because it had leaked so much.

There were further benefits. Heating systems could be reorganised and tanks removed. This improved efficiency and freed up important space for developing valuable rooms.

Access

Another remarkable change, entirely beyond our control, was the significant improvement to the regional road network. One of the reasons for closing the school in 1980 was its remoteness. The list of changes within the first 10 years of the new Centre was impressive. The M56 was completed in 1981, the M54 was extended in 1983, the Wrexham bypass opened in the late 1980s, the Oswestry bypass in 1986, the Chirk bypass in 1991, and the Shrewsbury bypass in 1994.

Together, these transformed access to The Quinta. Suddenly, with its substantially improved access to the North, Northwest, and Midlands conurbations and set in attractive countryside, one could even argue that The Quinta had become a prime location. These developments also made international travel considerably easier and increased the attractiveness of The Quinta for national conferences. The airports of Liverpool and Manchester are approximately an hour away, or just over. Birmingham is comfortably under two hours, compared to the three-hour car journey of only 20 years ago when Brett was brought to The Quinta by his social worker. (Chapter 6, 'Fruit in the Wilderness')

Another illustration of the crucial nature of physical resources is that there was a time, approximately twenty years into the Centre's life when OM began to consider the need to leave. This was when the chronic poverty of rural internet access had become so severe that it was becoming impossible for an international administration team to function. Staff had to work from home because, despite the tech guys doing everything they could, there was not enough internet capacity for everyone to work in the office. The cost of laying a cable was eye-watering, and the network capacity behind a new cable was struggling. Fortunately, the regulations changed just in time to allow cables to be run overground. The regional capacity also improved.

The Quinta has been blessed over the years. Our story can illustrate the history of transport from ancient drover trails and Roman roads, the coming of the canals and the railways, to the modern network of trunk roads and motorways.

It can also illustrate other themes of history with The Quinta estate having its own water collection system and reservoirs on the hills behind, culminating in the water tower at the front of Quinta Hall, to making gas on-site using coal from its own colliery, which was brought up by a horse-drawn railway and being the first property in the whole area to generate its own electricity. And it did not stop there. Quinta Hall and the former schoolroom buildings now have heating and hot water provided by new biomass boilers. The flat roofs of the Quinta Hall extensions have an array of nearly one hundred solar panels. About 130 years after electricity first lit up Quinta Hall, the estate was again generating electricity.

The Grounds

One of the great assets of The Quinta is its 52-acre parkland. It sits at the foot of the Welsh Hills and is on the spring line. The land can be quite wet sometimes, but it significantly extends the site's potential. In 1985, the grounds had been neglected for five years. Very early on, most of the main area between Quinta Hall and the lake and a field on the far side were ploughed and reseeded. Much of the parkland is recognised as an agricultural holding, so a regime was initiated allowing some of the land to be grazed for part of the year and used for leisure activities and camping at other times.

Around 3,000 trees and shrubs have been planted. The first planting filled in a series of otherwise dead corners around the estate. These included areas towards the bottom of the drive and some which border the bottom and top sides of the games field. They created sites for camps and caravans.

Ray and his wife, Vera, were some of the great characters at this stage of our story. Ray was the leader of the group that suddenly appeared in our first autumn and booked the derelict Quinta Hall for three weeks the following summer. Ray was a big man in every sense of the word: the kind of character who would not go unnoticed in a crowded room. His generosity and compassion were substantial.

Within a few years of their starting to use The Quinta for Tarsus Christian Holidays, Ray's business failed. To pay off their debts, they sold up and became homeless. I don't recall exactly how it happened, but they moved to Quinta Hall. There were several small rooms on the third floor. We expanded these to make a two-bedroom flat for them by adding another room in the roof space above the kitchen.

Getting a suitable beam in place to hold the floor of the new room was a memorable feat of ingenuity. Tom, the farmer with the grass-keep, helped us with an old JCB. This and various ladders and rollers enabled us to lift and push the rather large beam into position. We took great care. However, today, that would have been way beyond acceptable practice. The beam was initially bought for use at Cloverley Hall but became surplus to requirements. It was transported with a large part sticking out of the back of a van. To mitigate the hazard, they hitched up a trailer to the back of the van.

In return for the accommodation, Ray and Vera, and sometimes their grown-up family, would help us one day a week. On other days, they were market stall holders selling flowers and plants. They would be up before dawn to travel to the wholesale markets. They would give us lots of shrubs and some unusual saplings. Resident families would benefit from unsold bunches of flowers. Ray, especially, helped us with the first planting of trees. We tend to think trees grow slowly, but some of those planted then are now huge trees. I remember planting one by the main drive entrance. It fell in a storm at the end of 2024, having grown to 33 metres, over 100 feet tall. Ray and Vera also helped plant hundreds of daffodil bulbs. The ones at the main entrance are a delight in the spring. In 1985, there were very few flowers. Daffodils, snowdrops and primroses are far more prolific now, and more flowers are in the woods.

Buildings

If you are a glass-half-full person, you will see that the buildings are the site's most exciting asset. If you are a glass-half-empty person, you will realise that buildings are also a maintenance nightmare. There is the old Victorian Quinta Hall, with its crumbling limestone tracery windows, a range of poorly insulated 1960s designed buildings that are now all 60 years old and a miscellany of other stone and prefabricated wooden buildings. It can be dispiriting to sort one building out, while another falls apart behind your back.

There are different approaches to work on buildings. The key issue, of course, is money. If you can afford it, you tell an architect what you want, employ the best contractors and later the architect will give you the key. Then you walk into a pristine new building built and furnished precisely how you wanted it, with everything working. You are then free to get on with life largely unrestricted by maintenance issues. Thomas Barnes would have done this with Quinta Hall in 1856.

At the outset, OM depended heavily on the skills of its staff and volunteers to prepare its buildings for use. After Dantzic Street, anything would be an improvement. Still, after an intensive few months, it produced a suite of offices that could be the envy of a commercial organisation and serve it well for decades, with only minor upgrades needed. Gradually, the second block was divided into staff flats.

In 2005, some years after the large boilers and tanks had been removed, they decided to utilize that space and expand their offices to incorporate a meeting room that could accommodate up to 100 people. This triggered an interesting situation. Because they did not own the property, every improvement they made added capital value, not to OM but to Centre Ministries as the Trustees of the Price Trust. The minute a brick was laid, it was no longer theirs. Trustees are legally bound to manage their assets responsibly. As a result, Centre Ministries asked the Charity Commission for special permission to extend the OM lease to 35 years and provide side letters stating they would consider with favour granting another lease to OM. This enabled OM to use funds donated to them for this building extension.

Cause for Concern derived its funds from voluntary donations and income generated by its care services. Before the residents arrived, any home providing personal care had to be formally approved as suitable. Later, they added a modest extension to one of the bungalows and UPVC double glazing throughout.

Developing a 250+ Bed Conference Centre

For Centre Ministries, the reality was the opposite of the utopia of employing architects and contractors and picking up the keys to new buildings. They took on all the old buildings and all their problems. Rightly or wrongly, Centre Ministries, with few exceptions, subscribed to an ethic that held that Christian conference centre work should pay for itself. It should not draw from the pool of Christian giving, which the Trustees felt should be reserved for Christian mission and relief work.

This aspiration was combined with a second one: They also wanted The Quinta to be a low-cost facility for young people and less affluent groups.

The reality was that financial margins would always be low. The income generated would never be large enough to repay any significant capital investment. In human terms, this business model was hazardous, if not crazy.

Looking back, "crazy" might be a good word to describe the first decade of the new conference centre. It was a time of living with seemingly impossible situations. We existed outside the box of always making safe decisions. We had to take risks that involved a vulnerability to failure. But that was an exhilarating place to be, working with others in a shared exercise of faith, that to others might seem foolish. For the first year before opening, we survived financially on the back of the two other centres in the group, Cloverley Hall and Castlewellan Castle. Then, we depended on them for many years to sustain cash flow through the winter months as we borrowed money to fund ongoing building development. We earned it all back across busy summers, then started the cycle again.

It was a very disciplined approach, with spending strictly limited to predicted income in that financial year. The regime's frugality was often onerous to staff and the butt of jokes which were a touch too close to reality: like having to straighten bent nails! A lack of money usually means you must frequently take the long, hard road. With plenty of money, you can get the best materials and pay to take shortcuts.

Behind this are challenging philosophical and theological issues. In the long term, is it not more cost-effective to use the best materials? Isn't second-hand second-rate and not good enough for God? If you don't get the best, is it simply because you lack faith? Do you agree? Are you happy to tell single parents who struggle to finance their weekly shop at Aldi that they should shop down the road at Waitrose?

It is easy to look back and ponder the wisdom of past decisions. However, the testimony is that this investment approach has been successful despite all the complexities. An educated guess is that overnight stays at The Quinta during our journey were substantially over one million. This roughly translates to around half a million guests staying there. However, this figure is difficult to determine because many people stay more than once.

This "crazy" approach generated hundreds of adventures and a treasury of anecdotes for the dinner table. I can only pass on a few of these to give you the flavour of the intensive period of DIY building development. Breaking down the school dormitories in Quinta Hall into small bedrooms with washbasins was an early goal, as was the redevelopment of the area that is now the Quinta Hall dining room from school toilets, showers, boot room and sewing room. However, this paled into insignificance compared to the work that needed to be done in the former workshops and schoolrooms. All the buildings now known as the 'Severn Lodge' complex were virtually rebuilt inside. Disconnected areas had new connecting doors, and two completely new floors were added in two locations, accompanied by two new sets of stairs and an external fire escape. Three relatively small extensions were added.

Early on, we had a memorable visit from a group of volunteers from the USA that, in three weeks, helped create five bedrooms in what used to be a builder's workshop in the Quinta School days.

So many other things fell into place out of the blue. When we opened an early version of Severn Lodge, we had no money left over to carpet the unit. Littlewoods store in Oswestry announced that it was refitting its store, which had been recarpeted with high-quality carpet only a few years before. As an opportunist, I successfully negotiated the purchase of the carpet with the store manager. A week or so later, he phoned to tell me that the company had refused to let him sell the carpet to a charity. So, he had to give us all the carpet, except for some, which we re-fitted for him in an upstairs corridor. Almost from nowhere at the precise time of need, we had several thousand square feet of free, top-quality carpet that covered most of the Severn Lodge building. Much of this carpet still survives in lower-use areas like bedrooms nearly 40 years later.

This way of working depended heavily on the maintenance team's skills, ingenuity and hard work. The Centre owes a great deal to them. For some years, we had a notice on the office board reading: "We have done so much for so long with so little that we can now do almost anything with nothing!"

Alongside was another more common quotation: "The person who makes no mistakes does not usually make anything." Seeing the conference centre work develop and blossom with so many people using it was highly satisfying. We did remarkably little advertising, but we found that we had as many visitors as we could cope with over the early years: enough to fund the next round of development.

One of the more memorable adventures was the result of attending a big auction at a mental hospital in Gloucestershire that was closing. I went with a modest shopping list. I was shocked at the start by the price of some lots of stacking chairs. They sold for more than it would have cost me to have brand-new ones delivered. However, as the auction went on, there were some real bargains. Despite this, some of the things that interested me were not auctioned. For example, in the big central kitchen, there was an extraction hood that I felt we could use to develop the Severn Lodge and Annexe kitchens. I was told to contact the demolition contractors.

A week or so later, we were allowed to go in and help ourselves. Along with colleagues from Cloverly Hall, we took two large, hired box vans, our own vans and a box trailer. We spent a long day stripping out many useful things from this massive hospital. These included many good-quality lights and electrical fittings, including emergency lights.

Simple things included grab rails, usable signage, washbasins and a host of small fixtures and fittings.

Additionally, we took apart and bought back the large kitchen extraction hood now built into Severn Lodge. We also took a significant quantity of good-quality bedroom units finished in Formica with no handles. These were built into some of the bedrooms in Severn Lodge and the Annexe. We helped ourselves to the theatre curtains, which, though a bit worse for wear, still hang in the Sports Hall. We must have come away with thousands of pounds worth of kit. I confess that I overloaded the box trailer I was towing behind our van so much that I couldn't get going again when I stopped on the steeper part drive up to Quinta Hall to talk to someone.

Somehow, we managed to develop a large, six-unit residential centre without any fundraising or financial loans. It was fun, but sometimes hard at times. We did some things brilliantly and some things badly. Being part of something we all felt was much bigger than us was a privilege.

There was no lighting on the main drive. Being mindful of light pollution, we installed downlighters to provide enough light to show the way. We followed Thomas Barnes' example of building scripture into architecture. He even had the Lord's Prayer inscribed around the ceiling of the reception area in Quinta Hall. On the drive light posts, you can see a jumble of letters as though they had been poured out. There are nine posts. Spoiler alert: they each spell out one of the fruits of the Spirit Paul lists in his letter to the

Galatians. Starting from the top with love, joy and peace, guests can work out the names of the rest as they walk down the drive. As Paul makes clear elsewhere, you can have all the resources in the world, but if you do not start with love, your potential is untapped. This challenge is built into the fabric to encourage everyone to reflect.

PETER BEVINGTON

FREED TO SERVE

The journey now tries to capture the essence of The Quinta. What actually happens there?

A patchwork of the feelings and experiences of a few of those involved represent the hundreds of tales that could be told.

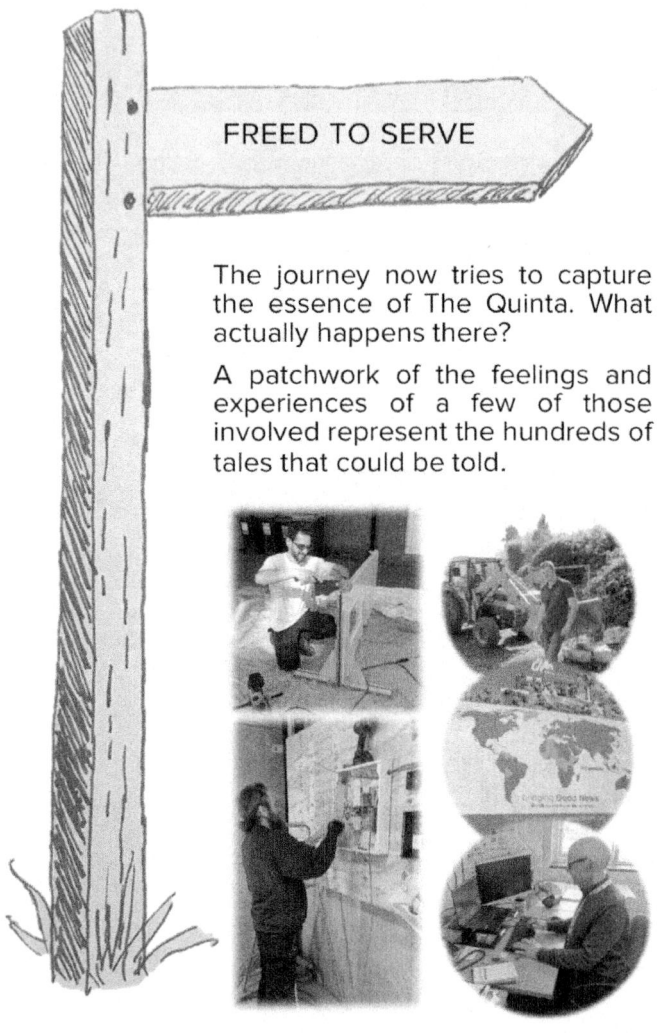

QUINTA TIMELINE circa 2000 2025

Chapter 10
Freed to Serve

The World of Operation Mobilisation

Modern missionary work has moved a long way from the times of Thomas and Ellen Barnes. Sometimes, those days are given a bad name by being superficially depicted as "mission riding on the coattails of the empire." Often, it was the other way around, with empire and commerce following missionaries. However, during the first part of the twentieth century, missions learned a lot more about the discipline of working in and with the cultures and languages of the people they wanted to influence.

This process has continued to blossom during OM's time at the Quinta. Mission work is now primarily focused on supporting nationals working in their own countries. The structure of the work is global and complex. It is often closely related to providing relief, training and other services. The presentation of the Christian gospel is as diverse as the world's cultures. It frequently involves partnerships and teamwork with other organisations.

Many countries are hostile to the Christian faith. Sometimes, ruling regimes and rebel fighters are actively engaged in persecuting Christian believers. This persecution is so widespread that Open Doors produces an annual World Watch List of the 50 countries where it is most difficult, and sometimes even life-threatening, to be a Christian.[31] OM is deeply involved in promoting and supporting Christian ministry directly or indirectly in many of these hostile environments.

OM UK's Annual Accounts for 2023 show a gross turnover of over £10 million.[32] As previously noted, OM Worldwide now operates in 145 countries with 4,500 staff members from 128 nationalities. Its two ships, Logos Hope and Doulos Hope, visit ports worldwide. Almost 400 staff members are from the UK and are deployed in approximately 50 different countries.

These realities are just amazing — stunning even. There can be a loss for words when placed in the context of the past. When you think back to the Barnes family's interest in the world mission or imagine Charles Price's vision to buy The Quinta for Christian use, who could have imagined what would happen? Put all this in the context of the time when all the plans for using The Quinta fell apart, only 40 years ago, and it is even more remarkable.

For such a large organisation, the OM UK team is relatively small. It encompasses all leadership, administrative, financial and promotional activities. Many staff work their way through the organisation, starting on short-term assignments. Others join the team later in life because of the skill set they can offer.

Steve helped me understand what it is like to work at The Quinta for an international mission, relief and training organisation. His house is in the village, precisely one mile from his office. He often walks to work through the village. He enjoys the beauty of the scenery as he walks up the drive to his office. As he enters his office, he explains, "It's like walking into the world." He becomes intimately involved with situations all over the world.

Steve first came to The Quinta during the opening months of 1987 to discuss with the UK team leader, Tony, what he should do next with OM. He had just spent two years working in the Indian subcontinent. During that time, he had met his future wife, Sandie, who had driven overland all the way to Calcutta from Belgium, where she had been working. They went their different ways but met again at an OM conference and were married in 1990. They then spent some years away from OM, but in 1996, with two children, they joined the ship MV Doulos and stayed for over three years. Then, they moved to Bangladesh, where Steve was the team's field leader, comprising two British families, six short-term workers and approximately 40 Bangladeshis. When they returned to The Quinta, like so many others who work there, they felt their life experiences had prepared them for their leading administrative roles. Steve now heads the Personnel Department. Sandie is the Director of Community.

George remembers joining OM in 1995. He arrived with a group of others during the night. George had come from Scotland, and his life was to change. He worked as the Mail Room Manager, sending material all over the world. It made him feel part of the worldwide scene. He remembers the depth of the relationships he has made over the years. Emotionally, it was hard to start with: he found sharing a flat difficult. Now, he has chalked up 30 years. He loves it and would recommend it.

One could tell thousands of stories to illustrate the OM work at The Quinta. At the memorial service for George Verwer, 1938-2023, the founder of OM, one speaker described George's influence on the Church in the Indian subcontinent in apostolic terms. For example, a decade or so ago, representatives of the Dalits, people regarded as "untouchables" outside the caste system, asked OM to assist with developing schools and churches. Much of this work was initially guided by a team at The Quinta. Hundreds of schools were created, and churches were founded relatively quickly. This had a significant impact on the Dalits, the outcasts and the lowest people in the caste system.

Behind the scenes, OM's move to the Quinta facilitated a lot of hidden infrastructure work. All UK charities faced a tsunami of change in regulation and expectation around the beginning of the new millennium. Christian missions were not exempt. For example, OM had to come to terms with tax regulations that meant they could no longer offer free accommodation in lieu of salary, except in very tightly controlled circumstances. Quinta OM staff found themselves having to pay tax on the rental value of the houses they occupied. All employment practices and policies had to be reviewed for this and other reasons. Like many other relatively young organisations, OM, founded in 1957, gradually realised they had employees approaching retirement who needed pensions and care as they transitioned from active mission work.

In addition, the last forty years have seen a digital revolution, which is now being followed at dazzling speed by the Artificial Intelligence revolution. OM has progressed considerably from the organisation that moved from Dantzig Street in 1985. It is immensely exciting. OM at The Quinta participates in a Global Day of Prayer each month and hosts an Internet global prayer meeting. Prayer is a foundation stone of their work.

The Conference Centre World

When I first met Alistair, I had become the Centre Ministries' first part-time CEO, a role previously held by the Chair of Trustees. We were interviewing for the post of Assistant Manager at Cloverley Hall. I'll never forget the shock on his face when I suggested to Alistair that he should have applied for The Quinta job (we were also looking for someone to take over my manager's role there). We persuaded him to look around on his way home. Alistair and his wife, Sarah, loved the feel of The Quinta but were slightly alarmed by the job description, having never worked in a similar residential centre before. Mike, who showed him around, told me he didn't think we would see Alistair again. But after prayer and wise counsel from friends and family, he returned for another interview. By then, Alistair and Sarah felt this was where God wanted them to be.

Sixteen years later, he reflected that his overriding conclusion was that "The Quinta is God's place". Time and time again, he had sensed an overall pattern in his Quinta journey: the crucial things fell into place. Resources, sometimes unexpectedly, would be available when needed. The right staff would appear at the right time. Even devastating booking cancellations would often be filled at the last minute. He shared, along with most others involved, the feeling that the purpose of The Quinta is greater than the sum of any individual's involvement.

He was encouraged that The Quinta is a memory-making place. A few visitors may not feel positive about their experience, but most regard The Quinta with deep affection. Some even use the language of coming home when they return. From the beginning, returning visitors have been a feature. As time passed, Alistair found that it was increasingly common for people who visited the Centre as children or young people to return decades later, bringing youth or church groups.

One of Alistair's most memorable experiences was the Pandemic in 2020. Working almost exclusively with groups of people, The Quinta was even more severely affected than others in the hospitality industry. The conference work shut down in March 2020. The three centres in the group were mothballed. They did not open fully again until July 2021, sixteen months later. You would be surprised to learn that they had more money in the bank at the end of the period than they did at the beginning. There was a wonderful response from both the staff and supporters. Being very resourceful, many of the staff found alternative work. Groups who used The Quinta were generous. These things made all the difference alongside the national Furlough Scheme and various government grants. As the lockdown eased a little, long before things returned to normal, a café catering to local people proved very successful. Some small holiday lets helped.

Centre Ministries deliberately chose to cater to Christian groups and a few others who, like some schools, accept its ethos. Charities can do this under an exemption to the Equality Act of 2010.[32] This means they cannot supplement income by advertising for commercial bookings at times of the year when voluntary groups do not frequently come away. This also means they can turn away groups whose views and aspirations contradict orthodox Christian teaching. This choice restricts its market potential.

The purpose of The Quinta, enshrined in the Price Trust, is the priority rather than cash flow and market economics. Despite this, The Quinta has hosted over 30,000 guest nights a year for many years. Since the Pandemic, this has risen again to around 35,000. This translates to around 12,000 resident visitors a year. That is not far short of half a million resident visitors since the Centre opened. Again, we can reflect how astonished Charles Price would have been if he had been told this would happen within ninety years of his decision to leave a small country house in trust for Christian use.

Mike's story reveals a brief but painful period set against the broader context of years of joy and deep satisfaction. Hopefully, you will have already absorbed the reality that The Quinta story is big, easily big enough to cope with the darker elements of life's realities. Being a full-time staff member on the conference centre team is undoubtedly a great privilege. Meeting many people and doing so many worthwhile projects is usually great fun. However, there are times when it is difficult. Relationships can get awkward. Such times should not be swept under the carpet: they are part of the fabric.

Almost by definition, if you have a small team trying to provide various services to a wide range of people, you will inevitably have individuals who do not naturally get along well together. It's not like a nine-to-five job where you can slam the door on Friday afternoon and walk away. Christians are expected to love one another. Most of the time, we accepted each other's differences lovingly and positively, but not always.

Mike wrote: "My first day at Quinta was memorable. The full-time staff met every weekday morning from 8:30 to 9:00 for Bible study, prayer, guest feedback and on-site work progress. Following devotions, I found myself ankle-deep in mud and water, preparing the foundations for a new shower room facility for the Annexe. I quickly learned a valuable Quinta principle: no materials were wasted, and even bent nails were straightened up for future use! Wherever possible, all work was done by qualified staff. This included grounds work, machinery servicing, electrical installation and boiler servicing. Finances were strictly controlled. This was fundamental to the success of the Centre. Work at The Quinta was varied. I was able to use my engineering skills: making large trash screens for the streams on the estate, fabricating steel site gates, making a suspension bridge across a tributary feeding the lake and helping with a total refurbishment of the Archway by fully plumbing the whole facility [toilets, wash hand basins, showers, the kitchen and the central heating].

The Lord answered many of our prayers and provided for our needs. One example was our need for meeting room chairs. We prayed during our morning devotions, and within a week, a telephone caller offered us 100 meeting room chairs ready for collection. There were many more examples.

The first five years of my employment were a challenge for me. One may be forgiven for believing that working on a beautiful Victorian estate with fellow Christians was bliss, but at times, it wasn't. There were many days I would arrive home and weep. It seemed that praying was not working. The atmosphere became so unbearable that it affected my standard of work and my relationships with colleagues, so I decided to leave my employment in June 2002.

I kept in touch with my ex-colleagues and learned that there had been staff changes and that staff relations had improved. In April 2003, I was re-employed and assigned duties on weekends, assisting the duty manager and supporting the guests. It was a humbling experience supporting group leaders and guests. These times reminded us of the value of our supporting ministry."

In 2009, Mike became the Maintenance and Development Manager. The Centre was maturing and reaching a new era of development. Mike was able to spend more time planning larger projects. He conducted a site survey and produced a document detailing the Centre's carbon footprint. The solar panels on the roof of Quinta Hall were followed by biomass boilers for Quinta Hall. Next was a completely new workshop complex, probably the best of any comparable Centre in the UK. At the same time, a small district biomass heating system was installed for the Lodge complex, which includes the upgraded swimming pool with its new PVC cover, sports hall, changing rooms and two staff houses.

Moving the workshops created space to improve the facilities at the Severn Lodge complex, introducing new kitchen, dining and meeting rooms for The Annexe.

Mike concluded his recollections by writing that his time at The Quinta "...was very satisfying. Just walking down the main drive and being reminded of the Fruits of the Spirit engraved on the lamp posts was special. Seeing the university students sitting on the lawn in small groups during the National Christian Student Leaders' Forum conference, discussing scripture passages and praying. Hearing guests and group leaders sharing their Christian experiences during their stay. There are many more. Perhaps the most notable words from many guests...'This is a very special place; we sense the Lord's presence here.'"

The room cleaning and checking team, on minimum-hours contracts, perform some of the most demanding and intensive work as they help turn the Centre around on changeover days by checking and cleaning the rooms. Sally, who had been on the team for 14 years, loves this work and spoke of her great relationships with her colleagues. The changeover days for a 285-bed centre, which can be divided into six separate units, generate a considerable workload. Approximately 80 toilets, 50 showers and over 130 washbasins require cleaning and sanitising. There are six sets of kitchens, dining rooms and additional meeting and ancillary rooms.

It is a highly disciplined and focused three to four-hour period. Many places of this kind require all guests to leave by 10 am or earlier and do not allow anyone in until 4 pm or later. The Quinta successfully adopts a very different yet flexible and disciplined approach, with varying times to vacate bedrooms, kitchens and meeting rooms. This allows groups to meet until around 11 am. Despite this, the units are ready for new guests by 2 pm. Credit for this goes to the hard-working staff for this guest-friendly approach.

Harry, Centre Ministries' current CEO, touched on many of these things, observing: "The Quinta has enjoyed a history of staff with a "can do" attitude in the face of limited finances and tight timeframes. They meet the "Immensity" of the place with "Ingenuity". The turnaround is constant. Maintaining and keeping these facilities safe is like painting the Forth Bridge. But, despite this, The Quinta has an "Intimacy"; it is a thin place for those needing to get close to God. So, for me, it is a place of "I"s. It's at its best when all the "I"s come together as an "us", raising the roof with a euphony of praise to the One who made it all—the Great I AM." (Exodus 3:14)

A Cause for Concern

This part of the story must include "A Cause for Concern". David, their Director, was interested in the potential of The Quinta from the beginning. Early in 1988, they opened the bungalows at the bottom of the drive as a care home for adults with learning difficulties. After just over ten years, the home closed, and Centre Ministries used the buildings to extend their conference centre ministry. The primary reason for the closure was the difficulty in finding adequately qualified senior staff. Even though they were doing well, official registration required the home to have leaders with the relevant qualifications. There was also an increasing trend for these homes to be even smaller and embedded in the Centre of a community, indistinguishable from the house next door. Cause for Concern changed its name to "Prospects". Later, in 2016, Prospects merged with the Shaftesbury Society.

So, was Cause for Concern's short-lived enterprise a

mistake? The answer must be an emphatic "No," accompanied by an adjustment in thinking about the nature of value. Value is primarily about quality, not quantity. All their residents came to The Quinta from long-term hospital placements. They moved to a completely different life experience, much closer to everyday normality. One of their staff, Anita, has fond memories. She learned a great deal from the residents, whom she valued highly. The more able ones who went on to live independently became familiar figures to all at the Centre. Everyone was sad when they left.

Peter became Head of Occupation for them in 1988 and remained in the position until 1993 when he was made redundant due to the charity's need to reduce costs. He utilized his considerable expertise in woodworking, pottery, printing and other crafts to enrich the lives of the residents.

Five years later, it was a joy to welcome Peter back as a member of the conference centre maintenance team, where he served for another 24 years, making a further outstanding contribution. He remembers a lot of work on doors. Fortunately, he enjoyed this work. There are hundreds of them. They needed repair, fitting and making up to fire safety standards. He reckoned he worked on over half of them. Just imagine how many millions of times people have used his work without giving it a thought. Surely, he deserves the humble yet crucial status, aspired to by the psalmist, of being a "doorkeeper in the courts of the Lord" (Psalm 84:10).

His own conclusion to his Quinta story aptly sums up this part of our journey:

"For me, The Quinta has been an important and large part of my working life, sometimes even a refuge when I had a period of anxiety and depression. I will always be grateful that God took me there. I know I was where He wanted me to be."

PETER BEVINGTON

A CAST OF THOUSANDS

There is now a cast of thousands, if not millions, if you include those touched directly or indirectly by the work of O.M. across the globe.

The final part of the journey highlights a few of the stories of The Quinta guests.

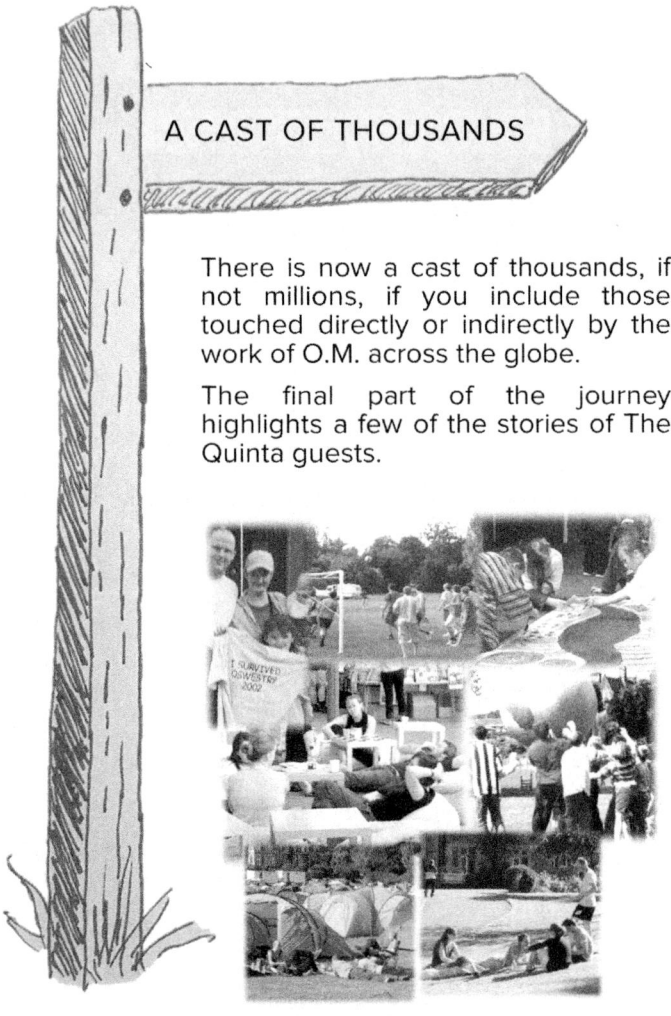

QUINTA TIMELINE circa 2000 ....

Chapter 11
A Cast of Thousands

With just over half of its guest accommodation deliberately geared towards young people, it is unsurprising that students are an important part of the Quinta family. A strong partnership exists between The Quinta and the Universities and Colleges Christian Fellowship [UCCF]. It stretches back over 30 years. In the early 1990s, The Quinta became home to their annual national training conference for student Christian leaders, Forum. In these early years, they stretched the seating capacity of the Sports Hall. This meeting venue severely limited the Forum's growth. So, one year they tried a university campus venue. It failed to create the warm cohesion and atmosphere they had grown used to at The Quinta.

So, they came back and asked how many people we could take. The answer was: "How many can you bring?" In addition to more than 250 beds, The Quinta has about 30 acres of grassland that are flat enough for camping. From this discussion, a creative partnership emerged. Forum immediately returned, and both organisations grew together. Forum today is a well-polished logistical exercise using facilities that have been gradually developed on-site and those that still need to be brought in. Students can buy into the conference at various levels, from self-catering camping to full board. Forum now hosts between 1,000 and 1,500 people for five days at the beginning of each academic year.

Of course, there are a multitude of anecdotes. One year was horrendously wet. The marquee was literally running with water. The carpet, supposedly covering the ground, was smelly and squelched in the mud. It was a nightmare. Yet, like so many other years, I think it was declared one of "the best ever". The quality of teaching, learning, fellowship and worship at Forum is always fantastic. It's a joy to witness this event playing a key role in encouraging, training and enabling Christian student leaders to pass on vision and encouragement to thousands of other students across the UK.

Water for Forum was an issue in other ways at other times. 1,000 plus people going to the toilet and having showers in the morning would lead to residents around The Quinta not having enough water in their homes. The mains system at that time could not cope. The first attempt to solve this problem was to hire a large articulated water tanker and fill it with water overnight for use during peak times of the day. Then, a staff member came up with the idea of removing the swimming pool from use and converting it into a storage tank for water used in showers and toilets on the main field. This worked well and saved the cost of hiring a tanker for the week.

Since then, the water pressure in the area has improved, but the swimming pool remains a backup. It became useful several years later when there was a desperate water shortage. They eventually discovered that the water company, for some inexplicable reason, had replaced the large commercial-sized meter for the site with an ordinary, small domestic meter during some repairs and mains renewal work.

Over the years, The Quinta has hosted numerous university Christian Union house parties from many universities in central England and beyond. The list includes large and famous universities, such as Oxford, Cambridge, Birmingham, Manchester and Warwick, as well as small, less well-known colleges. The house party season stretches from mid-autumn to mid-winter. A precious memory was watching coaches arrive one after another on a Friday evening to disgorge their contents: eager and enthusiastic young people. Then, on a Sunday afternoon, up to five coaches could be lined up behind Quinta Hall for the return journey.

Tim joined UCCF in 1989 and currently serves as the Field Director. He must have visited The Quinta well over a hundred times. He wonders how many tens of thousands of students have benefited from their time there, learning about and deepening their faith and how to share this with others.

Tim's most striking recollection is that Forum has been the launch pad for UCCF's three-year cycle of promoting one of the gospels. In the early days, they aimed to distribute as many gospels as possible to students across the UK, printing around 400,000 copies to give out free of charge.

In 2011, they changed their strategy and started producing the 'Uncover Gospels'.[34] The aim was to encourage Christian students to share the readings with their fellow students. The 'Uncover Gospels' are produced as high-quality hardback pocketbooks. They are designed with considerable care and research to be attractive and interact with the current student culture. They are backed by an impressive bank of digital resources. Usually, about 100,000 are produced. They are launched at Forum for the new generation of student Christian leaders to promote and use. 'Uncover Gospels' have been translated into more than 20 languages and circulated worldwide. There are many stories of students coming to faith in Christ through studying an 'Uncover Gospel' with a Christian friend.

Tim also highlighted another strategic event at The Quinta, UCCF's summer orientation training week. In 2009, they initiated summer programmes involving student teams working at various venues worldwide during summer vacations. These initiatives are similar to OM's short-term volunteer schemes, which are based at The Quinta.

The story of how Dave came to work at The Quinta in 1993 is another remarkable tale. The brief headline was that he was deeply disappointed by failing to obtain an earlier Quinta job that he had felt should have been offered to him. This pain was only relieved a year or so later when he was invited to lead the Maintenance Team, a role much more suited to his experience and abilities. A few months after starting this role, Dave led his final annual

Evangelical Movement of Wales Quinta summer camp with his wife, Pat and others. The camp drew around 50 young people, many of whom were not Christians. He writes: "A typical day would begin with a camp service at which the chaplain would speak. The rest of the day would be filled with various activities. In the evening, we had dormitory Bible studies. After the camp service, there was a day trip to Chester on Thursday. The chaplain preached powerfully, and we detected something special happening. Usually, campers would be off like a shot after the service, but this time, nobody moved. Heads were bowed with tears running down cheeks...the team included. This was no emotional event; it was a wonderful work of God's amazing grace. Campers took hymn books to the coach without any prompting and sang all the way there and back. Bible studies in the evening were more about the significant numbers that had come to faith, sharing their new life in Jesus. None of us wanted the camp to finish on Saturday. This was a fantastic time for us at the start of our service to God in our work at The Quinta."

Many organisations and churches come year after year. A very high proportion of visits are repeat visits. A special effort is made to support this reality. Bookings are only normally allowed three years in advance. Every January, the book for advanced bookings is opened. For example, in January 2025, bookings for 2027 are made available. Regular users are offered a reservation without a deposit; only a commitment to attend is required at this stage.

But they must confirm their 2026 reservation. The system works well and protects loyal members of The Quinta family. Long-term relationships are built.

This means that many churches see The Quinta as their special place. This is great because The Quinta does not belong to its residents and staff: it was left in Trust for the Christian Community. Therein is a profound reality. Staff are merely stewards of The Quinta's inheritance. Therefore, in the 'Handbook for Leaders of Groups', this is spelt out: "As visiting guests, you are welcome to use and respect The Quinta as though it were your own." Rules are minimal to ensure physical and social safety. An example of this ethos is the guidance about noise: "You can keep yourself awake all night, but please keep your own noise within your buildings between 10.30 pm and 8.30 am."[35]

This is relevant because of the diversity of visitors to The Quinta. Many British ethnically orientated churches deeply value the self-catering element. They can live in harmony with the rhythms of life that bring them peace. They can eat their own food and freely express their own culture. These groups have taught me so much over the years and exposed shameful prejudices. For example, the leaders of one group were often in bed well past mid-morning, but their meetings would last well after midnight. One group did not even use the bedrooms but used other rooms as make-shift communal, single-sex dormitories. They provided an amazing example of commitment to prayer. Many of these visitors came from countries deeply hostile to Christianity and have a deep, practical, personal faith shaped by this experience.

Of course, amongst the many visitors, there have been those for whom The Quinta was not a good experience. Some may have falsely believed they would enjoy the best possible five-star accommodation. They would have been disappointed by the more moderate Quinta provision. For others, my colleagues and I may have made mistakes which spoiled their stay. Others might have been dealing with painful personal issues that remained throughout and after their stay. A few groups may have brought with them church or organisational problems that worsened rather than improved. This is the nature of real life.

In a slightly different category was a week that none of those involved will ever forget. The Free Church of Scotland has had summer camps at The Quinta for over three decades. Teenagers come from remote Islands and the Highlands. For them, the holiday highlights are shopping in Chester or at the Cheshire Oaks Retail Outlet. They enjoy days out at Alton Towers and other places and experiences that their remote homes, situated in places of great beauty, cannot provide.

One year, someone with a norovirus-type infection boarded the bus, probably where the journey began at the ferry terminal for the Islands. The virus spread over the next 10 hours as the bus meandered across Scotland, picking up people. Several days into their stay, many of them started vomiting all over the place. I was called across in the evening to help. It just got worse. I decided not to stay but to divert my energy to get up early to help sort things out.

Early in the morning, I found a shattered leader. Twenty-three people had been admitted overnight to the nearest hospital in Wrexham, over the border in Wales. Not so much was known about the virus in those days. With everyone going sick simultaneously, it mimicked a severe case of food poisoning. The actual cause emerged during the day. Another member of staff and I were immediately quarantined and left to deal with the group. Meanwhile, the other staff kept the rest of the Centre's work going. We quickly learned about sanitising a building, including the correct procedures to follow and chemicals to use.

So, their holiday was devastated. A couple, with a small child, who were doing the catering left immediately for their child's safety. Half the leadership had been sick, and the remaining small leadership team had to manage everything, including the catering. They had to leave a day early so we could sanitise the building. They produced a T-shirt with "I Survived Oswestry 2002" emblazoned on the front.

There were some noteworthy consequences. Wrexham Maelor Hospital had to clear its surgical wards for a few days, resulting in the cancellation of planned surgery. They were not amused. These Scots visiting England had created havoc in Wales. A high-level international health meeting was called at The Quinta!

As it happened, Adventure Plus were providing an activity programme for the Free Church camp. Immediately afterwards, those A+ staff were going to join a larger team to provide activities for a large school group. They had to withdraw from this because they were still potentially contagious.

Given the circumstances, it was decided at the last minute to move the venue for the school to Cloverley Hall. Martin, Quinta's Schools' Worker, had to load our van with all the kit and all the catering supplies to take it to the new venue. As can only happen on such stressful days, the diesel van was refuelled with petrol on the way! The school week went very well, with one exception. With all the frantic rearrangements, they forgot to notify the local gamekeeper of their fireworks on the last night. Unfortunately, a pen of pheasant chicks suffered mass panic. Many died. So, the headline in the following Quinta News Sheet was "Over 100 dead and 23 hospitalised".

Fortunately, that was a once-in-a-lifetime event. The routine is to receive good feedback, testifying to positive experiences. The following memory is typical:

"Quinta was our annual church family week away! We counted the days down to it as the best location to spend a weekend with our church family, having the greatest of times! For years, we would spend every May at the big house. The youth group sessions moved to the main sessions as we got older. The group meals, the scrummy breakfasts, the excitement of the tuck shop! Every Saturday evening, we would have a line dancing up in the Sports Hall, a talent show, or a quiz night. The laughs we had at these events. I could put myself right there again in an instant."

"We always came away sensing God's presence, feeling incredibly blessed to belong to such a great family and having memories and stories to share at school on Monday! I often laugh and say I'd love to have a reunion now, especially since we've all grown up, gotten married, moved away and started our own families. Quinta, you were and always will be a huge part of my childhood. Thank you."

Sometimes, exceptional individual experiences stay in the memory. Many romances have blossomed at The Quinta. I remember meeting someone for something unrelated to The Quinta and being immediately told: "I met my wife at The Quinta." There was the time when a church group went on the traditional Quinta Walk down into the Ceiriog Valley, over Pontfaen Bridge, into Wales, past Chirk Castle gates, back through the Chirk Tunnel and across the aqueduct. A guest knelt midway across the aqueduct and proposed to his girlfriend.

It was not unknown for guests to be baptised in the lake even in mid-winter. Another guest wrote, "I attended a church weekend away at The Quinta. On 7 April 2019, I was baptised in the swimming pool alongside my twin sister and two other church members. The weekend was Spirit-filled, with joy and encouragement." Fortunately, the swimming pool is now covered, heated and more suitable for baptisms.

It is wonderful that The Quinta hosts life in its rich variety and serves as a venue that inspires many to grow into a personal fullness of life, as its current publicity declares: "The Quinta: Space to Grow."

Epilogue: What's In A Name?

Seasoned believers will know something of God's supreme sense of humour delivered with sharpness but in compassionate love. I was proud of my success with garden produce at the now-defunct Weston Rhyn Show. I was pleased with the admiration of the Black Hamburg grapes I had grown at The Quinta. You can imagine how I laughed at myself when I discovered that Thomas Barnes, well over a century earlier, had won prizes and specific commendations for his Black Hamburg Grapes at the Royal Horticultural Society show in London.

Then there were the OM staff's prayers in their pathetic accommodation at Dantzig Street — prayers that evolved into listing their fantasy desires for their new location, only to discover, to their amusement, almost immediately afterwards, that their new home even had space for the team member's pony.

There was also Charles Price, who bought the Quinta for Christian use, hedging his bets by saying that if no use was found, then it was to be sold with half of the money going for work in China: only for Quinta Hall to end up with its first guests being Chinese and their speaker a former leader of mission work in China

In the spirit of divine humour, I conclude with a somewhat absurd yet tantalising suggestion. During my research into the name "Quinta," I came across the old-fashioned Spanish word "quintar." It had military connotations and was variously used in the context of calling up, conscripting and drafting.[36] So, here's a brand-new, tongue-in-cheek theory. I suggest that the name, whatever its origin, was a prophetic statement predicting that The Quinta would ultimately become involved in calling people up, mobilising, training and sending them out equipped to serve.

Chapter 12
Fireside Reflections

Many share the memorable experience of sitting at the Quinta campfire site by the lake. I have, therefore, called this concluding part of the journey 'Fireside Reflections'. It enables me to share my personal thoughts about The Quinta's history.

Putting This Guide Together

I have always had a sense that the exact content of this journey was not completely in my control. Research would require that I share what I discovered. The stories I invited from others would set their own tone. I set out with a working title, 'A Place and Its People.' However, what emerged made this title increasingly inadequate.

Any good work of art or literature possesses a vibrancy within itself that connects and resonates not only within itself but also with life. The story of The Quinta ticks all the boxes to such an extent that some of the stories within the overall narrative are stranger than any work of fiction. But it is not a work of fiction. The authenticity of the story means that it contains true-to-life insights and patterns that challenge and encourage me as I try to make sense of life's events.

My concept of eternity may be off the mark, but

mistakenly or otherwise, I look forward to talking to many of the characters encountered on this journey. Just imagine having a chat with Charles Price. Finding out how he reacted to what happened 50 years after he died. There is no other word to use than "incredible" to describe how such a small place could be transformed, at no expense to his Trust, into a large centre of national and international influence. Given Charles' support for mission work in China, I would also love to know how he felt about the stunning fact that the first guests at the new Quinta Christian Conference Centre were Chinese. I'd like to ask whether he actually knew or was aware of their speaker, Dr. Leslie Lyall, who went as a young missionary to China in 1929, towards the end of Charles' life.

The Central Issue: Credibility

Unless this whole book is a cynical hoax and the string of "coincidences" featured are lies, the story of The Quinta has serious implications because it defies the statistical laws of probability. It undermines the widely held opinions that life is random, and that God is a delusion. Those opinions are not credible if the stories are true. They leave me unable to come up with a rational explanation of events other than that God exists. Not only that, but God constantly interacts with the damaged and difficult world we encounter. The Quinta journey has been about God. It has been a privilege to try to communicate this profoundly important message.

The Implications

This conclusion leads me to take seriously the account of God revealed in the Bible. The overall message is that God offers everyone an intimate, eternal relationship with Him through the death of His Son, Jesus. This, like so many other mysteries, is beyond my full understanding. I still have questions when I consider the horrors of our broken world, even though a thorough reading of the Bible provides insights into the dynamics of that brokenness and puts it in the context of eternity and God's offer of healing and wholeness.

Sadly, many miss out on the opportunity to experience what sometimes seems like a parallel universe: the personal work of the Father, the Son and the Holy Spirit in their lives. This "supernatural" reality is amazing. It is available to everyone for the asking. God promises to reveal Himself to those who look for Him (Jeremiah 29:12-14, Matthew 7:7)

But I am forced to ask myself how deeply do I really absorb these principles? So often, I drift towards the point where the truth is that I slip into living my Mondays as though God does not exist. Faith is often too easily boxed away in routine religious activity. The Quinta story demonstrates that God is present in both the details and the broad sweep of history.

If I truly believe this, it should be woven into the fabric of my personality and everyday life.

An Unbelievable Inheritance

As I searched for a more appropriate title for this journey, I was reading through Paul's letter to the Romans. As you probably know, it is a closely argued, intellectual letter that explores the concepts central to the Christian experience and thinking. I recommend reading Peterson's free translation, 'The Message,' because it cuts through some of the complicated sentences and jargon. His comments in the Devotional edition are particularly helpful.[37] Chapter 8 deals with the wonderful experience of being a Christian.

The phrases Peterson uses describe Christians being led by God into "a spacious free life" and experiencing "God's action in them". He sums up the words of the more accurate and precise translations that talk of Christians not only being "children" but also "heirs of God" by using the phrase, "an unbelievable inheritance". Although Paul was attempting to describe the reality of the ordinary Christian's experience, this phrase also described The Quinta story so well that it became the natural title for the journey.

Paul acknowledges the difficulties and intractable problems of life. In this context, we aspire to embody the message of the light posts on The Quinta drive: to grow in the fruits of the Spirit, which are love, joy, peace, patience, kindness, goodness, faithfulness, gentleness and self-control. This aspiration is in stark contrast to our society's self-centred values and hype. My generation has led the way in an unprecedented promotion of the "religion of self": self-confidence, self-esteem, self-actualisation, self-care, self-help, self-promotion and self-identity. Media of every kind provide a constant deluge of advice on how to look after and improve oneself. However, does this focus on "self" lead to a world broken by my own and others' selfishness?

Christ's own teaching presents a parallel path to self-fulfilment that is utterly different. His love for all individuals is his supreme driving force but look closely and you will see that his teaching takes a unique approach. Jesus presents a vibrant countercultural message that offers so much when self-care fails, and despair and hopelessness prevail. Blessing lies not in being strong, but in embracing weakness and accepting what God has to offer and what He does. It can even lie in self-denial and suffering. Mysteriously, it is in these ways that the unique "self" that God intended for each person emerges.

In Matthew's great summary of Jesus' teaching, known as the Sermon on the Mount, Jesus pinpoints the mystery of living in God's blessing. I conclude with this because the fundamental message of 'An Unbelievable Inheritance' is about being involved with God and what He does, both in the grand scheme of things and at the personal level. How do I open myself to God so that He can develop the fruits of the Spirit in me, leading me to that self-fulfilment and wholeness that He desires for us?

I have again chosen The Message as a free

translation because I want those familiar with the more accurate, orthodox texts to ask themselves to what extent The Message captures the essence of what Jesus said and how that affects their daily life. I pray that this key to God's counterculture will linger in your minds and that the journey will bless you.

"When Jesus saw his ministry drawing huge crowds, he climbed a hillside. Those who were apprenticed to him, the committed, climbed with him. Arriving at a quiet place, he sat down and taught his climbing companions. This is what he said:

You're blessed when you're at the end of your rope. With less of you, there is more of God and his rule.

You're blessed when you feel you've lost what is most dear to you. Only then can you be embraced by the One most dear to you.

You're blessed when you're content with just who you are—no more, no less. That's the moment you find yourselves proud owners of everything that can't be bought.

You're blessed when you've worked up a good appetite for God. He's food and drink in the best meal you'll ever eat.

You're blessed when you care. At the moment of being "care-full," you find yourselves cared for.

You're blessed when you get your inside world—your mind and heart—put right. Then you can see God in the outside world.

You're blessed when you can show people how to cooperate instead of having to compete or fight. That's when you discover who you really are and your place in God's family.

You're blessed when your commitment to God provokes persecution. The persecution drives you even deeper into God's kingdom. Not only that—count yourselves blessed every time people put you down or throw you out or speak lies about you to discredit me."

Then, Jesus immediately challenges his followers to be light and salt in their neighbourhoods. Entering this world, as described by Jesus, is not unlike entering a parallel universe. It is one deeply committed to life's realities. It is not without problems and pain, but as many of those touched by The Quinta's ministries can testify, there is an underlying peace, joy and hope. These are expressed in a "can-do" attitude to life based on confidence, not in ourselves, but in God (Philippians 4: 12-14).

This is the unbelievable inheritance open to all.

AN UNBELIEVABLE INHERITANCE

References

1 Operation Mobilisation. [Online]. Available at: https://www.uk.om.org/ [2025/02/18].

2 The Quinta Christian Conference Centre, Centre Ministries. [Online]. Available at: https://www.quinta.org [2025/02/18].

3 Hurdsman, C.N. 2004. A History of the Parishes of St. Martin's and Weston Rhyn. (Wrexham: Bridge Books, 2004), p. 99.

4 Roman Britain. "Rhyn Park Forts." [Online]. Available at: https://www.roman-britain.co.uk/places/rhyn_park [2025/02/01].

5 HistoryPoints.org, Battle of Crogen Site, Castle Mill. [Online]. Available at: https://historypoints.org/index.php?page=battle-of-crogen-site-castle-mill [2025/02/01].

6 Evans, G. The Lords of Ruthyn. Ruthin Local History Society. [Online]. Available at: https://www.ruthinhistoryhanesrhuthun.org/the-lords-of-ruthin [2025/03/20].

7 Records of Ruthin Castle Estate (1604-1949) Denbighshire Archives. [Online]. Available at: https://denbighshirearchives.wordpress.com/wp-content/uploads/2013/06/ruthin-castle-collection.pdf [2025/03/20]

8 Curry, R.C. 2009. The Wild West Show: A Story of the Cornwallis-West Family. (Christchurch, Dorset: Natula Publications, 2009), p. 52.

9 Curry, R.C. 2009. The Wild West Show: A Story of the Cornwallis-West Family. (Christchurch: Natula Publications, 2009).

10 Ruthin Castle Conservation Trust. 'Welcome to the Historic Ruthin Castle. The Cornwallis-West Era' (leaflet, Ruthin Castle Hotel & Spa, North Wales, United Kingdom, March 2025).

11 Solicitors Longueville & Co of Oswestry. 'The Last Will and Testament of William Cornwallis-West of Ruthin Castle Denbigh, Esq. Member of Parliament' (will, Oswestry, United Kingdom, 1892).

12 Barnes, J. Thomas Barnes of Farnworth and The Quinta. A Chronicle of a Life 1812-1897. (Weston Rhyn: Quinta Press, 2012).

13 Barnes, J. Thomas Barnes of Farnworth and The Quinta. A Chronicle of a Life 1812-1897. (Weston Rhyn: Quinta Press, 2012), p 57.

14 Account of Labour and Materials Supplied in the Erection of The Quinta Sunday School for Thomas Barnes, Esq. J.P.' (transcription).

15 Barnes, J. Thomas Barnes of Farnworth and The Quinta. A Chronicle of a Life 1812-1897, (Weston Rhyn: Quinta Press, 2012), p. 72.

16 Bevington, P. Ellen Barnes Charitable Trust History. [Online]. Available at: https://www.ellenbarnescharitabletrust.org/charity-history [2025/02/04].

17 Barnes, J. 'The Barnes Family: James Richardson and Ellen Barnes' (unpublished work).

18 Clair, H. 'The Farnworth of The Past', The Farnworth Journal, Friday, 15 March 1935.

19 Bevington, P. Ellen Barnes Charitable Trust History. [Online]. Available at: https://www.ellenbarnescharitabletrust.org/charity-history [2025/02/04].

20 'The Oswestry Institute Fete', The Oswestry Advertizer and Montgomeryshire Mercury and Local Journal for the Borders of Wales, 16 August 1871.

21 Frith W. Letter to Harold Barnes, 20 November 1928, (transcript, supplied by Barnes, J.).

22 Bevington, P. Ellen Barnes Charitable Trust History. [Online]. Available at: https://www.ellenbarnescharitabletrust.org/charity-history [2025/02/04].

23 Leishman, Sir James. 'Tribute to the Memory of Mr C.E. Price, Edinburgh Ex-MP', Edinburgh Evening News, 9 July 1934.

24 Davies, Rev. R.G. 'Edinburgh Pulpit Tribute', Edinburgh Evening News, 9 July 1934

25 Mytton-Davies, 'C. Border Portraits', Oswestry and Border Counties Advertiser, 1 June 1956, p.6.

26 Casper, B.A. Reason for Living: A Story That Shocked the World, (Birmingham: Defiance Publishing, 2013).

27 Morris, D. 'Quinta Boys Reveal Hidden Talents' 7 November 1979. Oswestry and Border Counties Advertiser. p.11

28 Kirkwood, A. 'Leicestershire Inquiry 1992', Leicestershire County Council, (inquiry, Leicestershire, 1993).

29 Wing Yui So. A Passion for a Greater Vision: The Role of Leslie T. Lyall in the History of the China Inland Mission / Overseas Missionary Fellowship. [Online]. Available at: https://sosir.org/sites/sosir.org/files/attachments/A%20Passion%20for%20a%20Greater%20Vision.pdf [2025/03/21].

30 The National Archives. Finnart House School. [Online]. Available at: https://discovery.nationalarchives.gov.uk/details/r/f22dcfd7-86e2-4def-b1bf-618708630351 [2025/03/21].

31 Open Doors. World Watch List. The Top 50 Countries Where Following Jesus Costs the Most. [Online]. Available at: https://www.opendoors.org/en-US/persecution/countries/ [2025/02/11].

32 Charity Commission Search Results. Operation Mobilisation. [Online]. Available at: https://register-of-charities.charitycommission.gov.uk/en/charity-search/-/charity-details/1008196 [2025/02/11].

33 UK Government. Equality Act: Guidance for Charities. [Online]. Available at: https://www.gov.uk/government/publications/equality-act-guidance-for-charities [2025/02/11].

34 UCCF The Christian Unions. Uncover . [Online]. Available at: Resourceshttps://www.uccf.org.uk/uncover/about/uncover-resources [2025/02/11].

35 Centre Ministries. Quinta Group Leaders Handbook. [Online]. Available at: https://www.quinta.org/wp-content/uploads/2019/12/2019-Handbook.pdf [2025/02/11]

36 SpanishDictionary.Com.Quintar. [Online]. Available at: https://www.spanishdict.com/translate/quintar [2025/02/11].

37 Peterson, E.H. 'Living in Us and Working with Us', (extract from an unpublished sermon).

Illustrations and Graphics

Except for one or two early photographs, all photographs are taken by the author who created the graphics with the help of local artist, Jennifer Muir. Assistance with some older pictures was received from Quinta Press https://www.quintapress.com/ and staff from Ruthin Castle Hotel & Spa https://www.ruthincastle.co.uk/

AN UNBELIEVABLE INHERITANCE

www.livetheflow.com

This simple personal website began in 2017 to share a special holiday with family and friends. It has evolved, and other journeys have been added. But it's not your usual travel blog. It aims to go a bit deeper than tick-box tourism. Pictures of the awesome and the ordinary should inspire and provide ideas for fellow travellers.

Apart from enjoying natural beauty and amazing things, 'Livetheflow' aims to be thoughtful. 'Reflection' pages explore the meaning of life and faith. The intentional imagery of rivers, water, walking and journeys pervades the site to stimulate reflection. What is living all about?

The Travel Blogs include visits to New Zealand and the USA, as well as a stop-off in Dubai. Perhaps more will be added.

'Livetheflow' now also serves as a platform for one-off topics and some thought-provoking discussions about Christian matters. Again, perhaps more will be added. Although it remains an amateur and uncommercialised site that receives intermittent attention, 'Livetheflow' should stimulate, inform, inspire and provoke.

Take a look!

Peter Bevington

AN UNBELIEVABLE INHERITANCE

About PublishU

PublishU enables you to tell your story or communicate your message by writing and publishing a book worldwide.

"I never thought I would be able to write a book, let alone in 100 days... now I'm asking what else have I told myself that I can't do that I actually can?'"

PublishU Author

To find out more visit

www.PublishU.com

Printed in Dunstable, United Kingdom